THE
VICTORIAN
MUSE

Selected Criticism and Parody of the Period

A thirty-nine-volume facsimile set
essential to the study of one of the most
prolific periods in English literature

Edited by
William E. Fredeman, Ira Bruce Nadel, John F. Stasny

A Garland Series

ANTI-MAUD

THE COMING K——.

EVERY MAN HIS OWN POET

Garland Publishing, Inc.
New York & London
1986

For a complete list of the titles in this series
see the final pages of this volume.

These facsimiles have been made from copies in
the Yale University Library.

Library of Congress Cataloging-in-Publication Data

Bennett, W. C. (William Cox), 1820–1895.
Anti-Maud.

(The Victorian muse)
Previously published in London, 1856–1877.
1. Parodies. 2. English poetry—19th century.
I. Murray, Eustace Clare Grenville, 1824–1881.
Comming K——. 1986. II. Mallock, W. H. (William Hurrell),
1849–1923. Every man his own poet. 1986. III. Title.
IV. Title: Coming K——. V. Title: Every man his own poet.
VI. Series.
PR1195.P27B4 1986   821'.8'08   85-25364
ISBN 0-8240-8623-6 (alk. paper)

Design by Bonnie Goldsmith

The volumes in this series are printed on
acid-free, 250-year-life paper.

Printed in the United States of America

A N T I - M A U D.

ANTI-MAUD.

BY

A POET OF THE PEOPLE.

SECOND EDITION ENLARGED.

LONDON:

L. BOOTH, 307, REGENT STREET.

1856.

TO THE READER.

"Anti-Maud" is not merely a *jeu d'esprit*, but something besides of a more earnest character. More than this the Author thinks it best not to premise, but would take this opportunity of disclaiming any intention of depreciating the Laureate's poetry, yielding as it does, for the most part, ever-new delight to all who have realized its beauty, and felt the grasp of its power on their hearts. "Amicus *poeta*, sed magis amica veritas."

ANTI-MAUD.

———◆———

1.

I hate the murky pool at the back of the stable-
    yard,
For dear though it be to the ducks and geese, it has
    an unpleasant smell ;
If you gaze therein at your own sweet face, the
    reflection is broken and marred,
And Echo, there, if you ask how she is, replies, " I
    feel very unwell ?"

2.

For there in the muddy slush a moistened body was
     found,
A lap-dog I gave to my wife—Oh, Pompey, who
     would have thought it!
Swollen and decomposed, and trampled into the
     ground,
With the collar around its neck, which it wore on the
     day I bought it!

3.

Did he drown himself there? Who knows? For there
     had been strong competition
Between an old parrot and him to obtain their
     mistress' love;
And he growled and snarled all day, with scarcely an
     hour's intermission,
Like a door that creaks on a querulous hinge, each
     time you give it a shove.

4.

And well I remember 'twas only a few nights ago,

As I mused o'er my beer at supper, and thought it
      extremely small,

The stifled whine of a fav'rite dog was heard in the
      kitchen below,

And sharp as a two pronged fork the parrot laughed
      out " Pretty Poll !"

5.

Knavery somewhere? Whose? You'll find in the
      Laureate's book

That we're all of us knaves, knaves, knaves, in the
      lower classes and upper;

And my poor little dog, as 'tis said by the crabbed
      old cook,

Dropped gorged from the shoulder of lamb which
      was meant for the servant's supper.

6.

Pompey, my joy and my pet, which struck all the
    beggars aghast,

Pompey, the dread of my friends, which snarled till
    they gave him a kick,

Pompey, the bore of the village which yelped at eacl
    carriage that passed,

Pompey, which playfully bit my wife's little toe to
    the quick !

7.

Dead, dead, Sir, dead. Bury him deep enough
    without fail,

Lest his ghost should haunt me every night, and
    rudely disturb my rest,

Dismally moan at the side of my bed, and wag a
    sepulchral tail,

When the daisy is winking its eye, and Orion
    sprawls in the West.

8.

And am I not—am I not since become foolishly
    maudlin, grimly splenetic ?

Will any one tell me what I must do, to give my
    spirit some ease ?

Calomel, calomel, Sir, will do it—or maybe a salt-
    spoon of tartar emetic ;—

Well, well, let me have out my say, and then I will
    take what you please !

9.

Shall I weep if my wine-merchant fail ? Shall I
    shriek if my butcher break down ?

Or the schoolboys at Rugby or Harrow be governed
    by rod or by birch ?

I can't make a crooked world straight. We must
    all of us look to our own,

And let him whom we don't like to name, catch all
    who are left in the lurch.

10.

The grub which was munching your wheat is
    munched, in its turn, by the rook,
The gnat which has bitten your nose, if you catch it,
    falls crushed to the floor,
The goggle-eyed, gluttonous carp, makes a leap at
    the worm on the hook,
And is rather astonished than pleased to find himself
    hoisted on shore.

11.

Why do they prate of the blessings of peace? Bloody
    war is a holy thing.
The world is wicked, and base, and vile—shall I
    show you a new kind of cure ?
Smeared with blood and with parents' tears call for
    Moloch, horrible King !
Let him trample to dust, with a brutal foot, whatever
    remains of good or of pure !

12.

For I trust, if the low-browed rogue with a ticket-of-
leave from the gaol,
Encountered the sergeant recruiting, in rainbow-like
ribbons arrayed,
He would clutch the Queen's shilling with glee, and
draining the dregs of his ale,
Declare that the sack of Odessa would be quite of a
piece with his trade !

13.

Wanted a quarrel to set the world straight, and cure
it by letting of blood !
We are sick to the heart of ourselves, I think, and
so we are sick of each other :
Rapine, and carnage, and rage would do us all
manner of good ;
Let Christian rise up against Christian, and brother
take arms against brother !

14.

Alas! since I pondered in grief on the corpse of
    my martyred dog,

The cells of my brain are dark. I think not, I
    feel not aright,

But peer at the world and its ways through a sickly
    November fog.

Let me brush it away whilst I can, and let in the air
    and the light!

15.

The world is wicked, and base, and vile—How was
    it before the peace?

Was it well in the good old times when savage war
    was abroad?

Did no one cheat in the glorious days? Did no one
    plunder or fleece?

Was the libertine checked in his foul career? Was
    the merry Atheist awed?

16.

Methinks there was crime, black crime in the heart
    of the land,
A dare-devil selfish spirit, a spirit lying and base,
Haunting the wretched minds of men who would not
    understand
How the just God waited calmly until they had run
    their race ;—

17.

Watched and waited during the night, till the dawn
    of another world
Should smite with its cold clear light on the culprit's
    shivering brain ;—
The mystic curtain of life for ever and ever be
    furled,
The awful goodness revealed at length,—the terrible
    guilt made plain !

18.

Who cared for the dear ones of Christ, the sickly and
    starving poor,

When the scent of blood-dripping war hung faint
    on the skirts of the wind ?

Like rotting sheep that crawl o'er the fog-bound
    swampy moor

Nibbling rushes and snakepipe, so they wasted and
    pined !

19.

To take up the cause of the poor, what was it but
    Jacobinical ?

Rich and respectable classes were not to be robbed
    of their pleasure ;

Worldly, incredulous, selfish ; heedless of others, and
    cynical,

Bloated swine in a perfumed stye so they wallowed
    at leisure.

20.

Is it not better now—after a forty year's canker,

A forty year's canker of blessed peace which has
  given us life and hope?

Do the choking weeds of lust and pride shoot faster
  now and ranker?

Or has not the wholesome grain found a freer soil
  and scope?

21.

Under the shadow of peace something was done
  that was good;

We tore out a bloody page from the book of our
  ancient laws;

We struck off a bitter tax from the poor man's
  scanty food,

And Justice bent down from her seat to give ear to
  the poor man's cause.

22.

Under the shadow of peace thickly began to a rise

Many a home for the working poor, many a school
and church;

Little it may be, but better than roasting our
enemies' eyes

With Captain Disney's patent, or sacking the town
of Kertch.

23.

Under the shadow of peace, the fetters fell from the
slave,

As dead leaves fall from a tree at the touch of an
autumn storm;

And we ceased to maltreat, as a worthless fool or a
knave,

The Christian who broke with the Church on a point
of doctrine or form.

24.

By the tranquil voices of Science and Art millions of
    minds were taught;

By the wide-working wheels of Commerce millions
    of mouths were fed;

Little it may be, but better than burning the stores
    we had bought,

And making a bonfire of Russian wheat which was
    meant to make English bread.

25.

There is much remains to be done, by thought, by
    word, and by deed,—

But a truth is present to cheer us, raising us up
    from despair;

We have feebly groped for the right; we begin to
    know what we need:

We dimly see through the shows of the world, how
    poor and naked we are!

26.

We were ignorant once—'twas the good old time
of the wars,—

We were busy, and little inclined on such sorry
matters to think;

We let out the fighting on niggard terms to soldiers
and kidnapped tars,

And smothered our cares and fears with mouthfuls
of victual and drink.

27.

We were ignorant once; we seem to be now less
blind;

We have had some leisure for thinking—leisure for
seeing and feeling,

For were we not something better—better in heart
and in mind,—

Should we hear a Laureate Poet to a nobler sense
appealing?

28.

He feels in himself a touch of the age, he breathes
    no diviner air,
Child of the times he borrows his cue, and is neither
    better nor worse;
Pity was stirring the hearts of some, and the Laureate
    takes his share
In the work begun, and the quickening faith which
    strives to abate the curse.

29.

Who clamours for war?—Is it one who is ready to
    fight?
Is it one who will grasp the sword, and rush on the
    foe with a shout?
Far from it;—'tis one of a musing mind, who merely
    intends to write;
He sits at home by his own snug hearth, and hears
    the storm howl without.

30.

I grieve that a noble soul should trudge on a beaten
　　road,
And a voice that can move the heart, a vulgar
　　war-whoop swell;
Hounding his brethren onwards, urging them on
　　with a goad,
To the smoking field of death, where the combatants
　　close with a yell.

31.

The widow kneels in a darkened room, stunned by a
　　sudden woe;
Weep if you can, — weep and pray: there is One who
　　is mighty to save;
She hears her little ones laughing, laughing and
　　prattling below;
Quiet and cold their father lies, far-off in a bloody
　　grave.

32.

There in the by-lane foul, where the air and the
    water is bad,
And fever is never away,—mother and child are
    crying for food;—
Drown the clamour with drums and fife! The
    sinews of war must be had—
Money and men, money and men; the poor man's
    earnings, the poor man's blood!

33.

Plenty of work to be done in the filthy and crowded
    street,
Where the light of the gin-palace flares in the hollow
    eyes
Of the girl, who has pawned her shawl that her
    starving child may eat,
But turns aside for a penn'orth of drink, to comfort
    her ere she dies.

34.

Plenty of work, where the children stare through the
      workhouse gate,

Crushed and stunted in body and mind, and doomed
      to steal or to beg;

Hatched into mendicant life by the blundering care
      of the State,

Fatherless, motherless children, paupers and thieves
      in the egg!

35.

Plenty of work to be done.   But how to be done and
      by whom?

Men's hearts are angry and hot.   We feast upon
      warlike scenes.

We listen all day for the clash of the bells, and the
      cannons' triumphant boom.

Our hands are full. We have wasted our wealth. We
      have neither the time, nor the means.

36.

Fever, and famine, and plague are a fine corrective
    check
To the growth of a growing race which threatens to
    be too poor,
But if some of the boasted skill and the wealth which
    we had at our beck
Could have saved but the life of a little child, did we
    well to withhold the cure ?

37.

Who are the friends of the poor ? The men who
    babble and prattle
About the Balance of Power, and the pomp and
    grandeur of war ?
Thousands of miles away from the rush and the roar
    of battle,
Sipping their Seltzer and Hock, and smoking a mild
    cigar ?

38.

Who are the friends of the poor? The writers
    without a name,
Who scribble at so much a column, whatever the
    editors please,
Working the many-mouthed bellows which blew up
    the war to a flame,
And pleading for rapine and blood, whilst they
    lounge in their clubs at their ease?

39.

The horse-leeches' cry is for blood. Let the soldiers
    rot in the trench,
Let them tumble in heaps, split and crushed by the
    screaming shell,
Let the poor starve by inches at home, in the heat
    and the stench
Of a plague-stricken town—so the war is pushed on,
    —all is well.

40.

What are we fighting for now? We have put the
Russian to rout,

Bearded him in his den, and swept his seas far and
wide.

We have passed a strong hook through the Muscovite's
snout,

Drawing him homewards—drawing him back o'er
the Pruth that he passed in his pride.

41.

Methinks we have done enough for that turbaned
goat, the Turk,

Who spits when a Christian meets him, and would
spit, if he dared, in his face;

Methinks we have done enough, for 'tis but a thank-
less work

To rivet with care on a beautiful land, the clutch of
a barbarous race.

42.

The sword is red to the hilt with blood. Widows
 and orphans weep.
Grief in the North, grief in the South, from the
 Ural range to the Ukraine plain,
For an army laid low in Crimean earth under the
 blood-stained heap,
Which day and night for twelve long months we bled
 and we toiled to gain.

43.

Methinks we have done enough, for the sake of a
 statesman's whim,
Floundering onward, drifting downward, reeling and
 staggering to and fro !
Our foot is on shifting sand, and the heavens above
 us are dim,—
Close the eyes and clench the teeth,—whither and
 wherefore, who can know ?

44.

Let the Czar relax his hold on the Turco-Christian
    race ;
Let the Czar withdraw his grasp from the throat of
    the Danube river ;
Let the Czar be pledged to maintain the Turk in his
    ancient place ;
Let the Euxine sea be free to the fleets of the West
    for ever.

45.

Methinks that this were enough ;—but those political
    worms
That work in the ground and burrow,—the sickening
    curse of the nation,—
The statesmen, as they are called, would haggle
    about the terms,
And din in our ears, from morning till night, the
    cuckoo clamour of " Limitation !"

46.

Whether they wag a saucy tongue, or stealthily
work with the pen,
There is blood on the heads of those who are fanning
the flames of war ;
Blood on their heads, and blood at their doors; the
blood of our own brave men,
The blood of the wretched serfs who fight for their
Faith and their Czar.

47.

Fling the dice with an eager hand.   We will stand
the chance of the throw.
If we gather our stakes, what then ?   Will it be for
our woe or our weal ?
Shall we rise from that ghastly strife better off than
our shattered foe ?
The festering wounds of a needless war sink deep,
and are slow to heal.

48.

Set the peaceful town in a blaze. Smite the Muscovite
sore.

'Twill goad him perchance to revolt. He may turn
in despair

On his Czar, and destroy all he loved in his blindness
before,

Till an "infant civilization" sink to rest in a wild
beast's lair.

49.

Blow up the dockyard. Shell the fort. Burn the
fisherman's boat.

War swallows up little and great. We cannot afford
to be nice.

But the shock of each blow which we aim at our
foeman's throat

Thrills through the heart of each English home. We
may win, but what is the price?

50.

The future is dark.　But, methinks, in the depths of
　　the cloudy space,
The spectral shapes of a mighty host sweep the skies,
　　and rush
With the rapture of eager hate to the shock of a
　　foe's embrace;
And angrily over the vault of Heaven spreads and
　　glows a blood-red blush;

51.

Sounds of anguish come on the gale, sounds of
　　mourning and woe.
Millions arise in their wrath.　They claim what they
　　deem their own.
Midst the wreck of a thousand homes, and a throne
　　laid low,
We sit and gaze on a world that is waste, and reap
　　the storm we have sown.

LONDON:
Printed by Schulze and Co., 13, Poland Street.

THE COMING K—.

A Set of Idyll Lays.

———◆———

LONDON.

—

1873.

THE COMING K——

THE COMING K——.

DEDICATION.

THESE to his memory—since he held them dear,
Perchance as finding there unwittingly
Some picture of himself—I dedicate,
I dedicate, I consecrate with smiles—
These Idle Lays.

       Indeed, He seemed to me
Scarce other than my own ideal liege,
Who did not muchly care to trouble take ;
But his concern was, comfortable ease ;
To dress in well-cut tweeds, in doeskin suits,
In pants of patterns marvellous to see ;
To smoke good brands ; to quaff rare vintages ;

To feed himself with dainty meats withal ;

To sport with Amaryllis in the shade ;

To toy with what Neræa calls *her* hair ;

And, in a general way, to happy be,

If possible, and always debonair ;

Who spake few wise things ; did some foolish ones ;

Who was good-hearted, and by no means stiff ;

Who loved himself as well as any man ;

He who throughout his realms to their last isle

Was known full well, whose portraiture was found

In ev'ry album.

     We have lost him ; he is gone ;

We know him now ; ay, ay, perhaps too well,

For now we see him as he used to be,

How shallow, larky, genial-hearted, gay ;

With how much of self-satisfaction blessed—

Not swaying to this faction nor to that,

Because, perhaps, he neither understood ;

Not making his high place a Prussian perch

Of War's ambition, but the vantage-ground

Of comfort; and through a long tract of years
Wearing a bouquet in his buttonhole;
Once playing a thousand nameless little games,
Till communistic cobblers gleeful danced,
And democratic delvers hiss'd, " Ha! Ha!"
Who dared foreshadow, then, for his own son
A looser life, one less distraught than his?
Or how could Dilkland, dreaming of *his* sons,
Have hoped less for them than some heritance
Of such a life, a heart, a mind as thine,
Thou noble Father of her kings to be—
If fate so wills it, O most potent K——;
The patron once of Polo and of Poole,
Of actors and leviathan " comiques ";
Once dear to Science as to Art; once dear
To Sanscrit erudition as to either;
Dear to thy country in a double sense;
Dear to purveyors; ay, a liege indeed,
Beyond all titles, and a household name,
Hereafter, through all times, Guelpho the Gay!

THE COMING OF GUELPHO.

THE COMING OF GUELPHO.

THE Georges Four, come from th' Elector's loins,
Left none of gender masculine to reign ;
And so, no Salic law forbidding it,
A woman reigned and made fair weather o't.

But, ere the Isles had settled down to this,
Storms social and political had been ;—
Barbarian rule, incursions of the Dane,
The Saxons beat by Norman dodgery ;—
And William,—the Norman people's William,—
Nobbling the little lot for self and friends,
They had it their own way. The oracle
Was worked full cleverly. Conservative
Card trick by Gorst no higher claims to praise.
Still Gurth was hard to beat. But one fine day
A Norman prince fused with a Saxon gurl,

Saving the bacon of both Churl and Knight.

Planta Genista, the name botanic

Of the Broom, became a later fashion :

Of this house, Edward did grand deeds of arms,

And the great Lords and Barons of his realm

He led to victory on many a field.

The Broom worn out,—used last by Crook-back
    Dick—

Soddened with blood of Roses Red and White,

Came a new man, more upright than the last,

For he'd been crooked both outside and in.

Thus Wales, whom England bagged some time
    before,

Did score a point thro' queenly widow's love,

And Owen Tudor stood, a king's granddad.

Llewellyn mollified, these Tudors ruled

Irascible ; heads chopped, ears boxed, and died.

Then came a race, Stewards of Scotland they—

Pedantic, Frivolous, and Monarchs False,

Keeping of many things of others owned,

But of their word keeping no count at all,

Till men grew tired of their falsities

And slew their monarch with an Aye ! and Axe.

No whitewash him will blanch nor ever clean ;

His guilt immovable by Faiths or Wills.

Then came for England's guidance such a man

As, when we want, we'll hope his like again ;

Storm-ruler ; of Ironsides th' inventor ;

He no " cheek " stood, nor did in any way

Indemnities propose, or claims admit,

Save such as could be answered with his guns.

'Twas a good game to play.   England was feared.

The old disorder changed ; yielding place to law.

But, like a bow too tightly, quickly strung,

The tension all too great destroyed the arch

So beauteous in beauty, strong in strength,

And the thing " busted," and did pass away.

They had another turn,—in luck were they,—

These Stewards ; but they couldn't hold their own ;

Or, rather, wanted more than was their own ;

Revived old practices, and did commit

Larcenies petty and of larger scale.

So that, at last, the land, being wearied

Of such performance, cast them out amain

And called in another, *not* a Steward.

He was a poor relation ; and he came

Willingly, hoping a situation

Permanent, and that his board and lodging

Would be found him ; so, he would gladly work,

Do all the kingdom wanted to have done.

And he did it, and did it well also.

William his name, a man of ditch and dyke,

A Dutchman, so to say.   Liked gardens prim,

And certainly could fight ; like all his race.

And this did England like.   Aye ! always has

Its warriors loved ; its fighters fêted,

Whether at Farnborough, with Christian-name

Of Thomas, surname Sayers, or the Boyne

With Orange William, him called " Yaller Bill."

The last bill paid, and passed his final act,

Anne came ; and glory wreathed her chaplets
green

For men of sword and pen. Great Marlborough

Won famous victories abroad, but hid

His head diminished under Sarah's frown.

This the Augustan age, and Sarah Anne's.

Scotland then knit with England into one,

And ne'er went bock agin to border frays ;—

Black Mail went out and the Red Mail came in.

Thus all our pretty islands under her

England had brought, and made a realm ; it rained,

However, mostly, in this one or that,

For ocean melancholy and Scotch mist

Were not as yet o'ercome. But over came

The Hanover Elector now ; First George

Whom the realm knew ; but not the last by three.

These followed one another, as each died ;

And when the four had gone, no fifth remained.

Small pity this, if more " first gentlemen

Of Europe " were to come, like George the Last.

The ship of state a sailor now commands,

And, when he to the summons strikes his flag,

A girl in teens doth fill the vacant post,

And, like the queens before,—Elizabeth

And Anne,—she makes herself a name of love

From the Land's End e'en up to John o'Groat's.

'Tis much too near the present time to write

What might be written, but be written wrong,

Concerning many people of the realm,

And many subjects, both of high and low.

But let us tell you now another tale.

A prince, of science master, as they say,

Died but of late, and sent a note to us

To hear him speak before he left his life.

Pale with a chalky paleness lay the great,

And, when we entered, told us he and C.

Had been engaged in buying property.

That a good spec for some one was in hand,

And wished he might have lived to see the same

Succeed, for his own sake and theirs whom he

Had trusted with his aims and ends therein.

Tin-tagel-by-the-Sea was pretty good ;

But this, a mine of wealth *above* the ground,

Above the groundlings too (he winced with pain) ;

Aye ! it will answer full the purpose meant,

Or would have answered, if I could have lived.

But much I fear me there may be a cry

I cannot stifle when I am no more,

And mourning is worn out upon my score ;

So I would have the thing all quiet kept,

No mention of it made, no writing seen ;

So that no tittle of the testament

Can ever show to prove how great a screw

I've been.   So it may pass without concern ;

And when the weighty matters of the State

Encumber men with thought, then I may hope

That none shall know about this stunning haul.

So it was promised, and his will was done ;

And so the people were—all satisfied and still.

They never knew how warm he was,—for them

And him, and all his kith and kin about ;

And only in that distant Western shire,

Where Arthur had his Knights of Table Round,

Did there some knowledge of these things creep out ;

But it was little, and not mattered much,

For they were far away, these men who knew,

And little known.   And little did men care.

So came the turn of him, the Coming K——,

Whose brand is Henry Clay, brave brand to smoke,

But not to smite—another one in store

(Trade mark triangular, 'twould cost a crown

To counterfeit) is Bass, X *calibre*.

HERAINT AND SHENID

HERAINT AND SHENID.

THE rich Heraint, a knight of Guelpho's Court,
With house in Curzon Street, and castle, too,
In Cornwall, near to fishy old St. Mawes,
A member of the Malborrow Club, and one
Of Guelpho's doughty Dinner-Table Knights,
Had married Shenid, Jones's only child,
And loved her better even than his beer,
And loved to see her dress in brave attire;
So let her run up bills at Gask and Gask's,
Pay Swan and Edgar well nigh daily court,
And be to Lewis an annuity.
And she, who, when he wed her, was quite poor,
With many graces dower'd and but one dress,
Full oft availed her of her husband's mood,
Array'd herself, and daily fronted him
In some fresh splendour; sheeny, shimmering silk,
That paled the peacock's tail; made opals blanch,

And robbed the duck's egg of its sea-green tint.

At Hurlingham, at Chiswick, in the Drive,

At Goodwood, loved of lordlings and their loves,

She was, by one consent, the loveliest.

And such her charms and gracefulness that e'en

The mighty Dame of Cottonopolis,

Then high in favour with the Coming K——,

Was envious, made much of her, and oft

Would call her " dear," and squeeze her little hand ;

Would ask her, with much fervour, to the Mall ;

And then would rail at her, behind her back,

And to the ear of Guelpho call her " minx ! "

Her seeming love at first rejoiced Heraint,

But when a rumour rose about Her Grace,

Touching her love for cigarettes and " cups " ;

When it was whispered she did not eschew

The doctrines that Miss Woodhull had proclaimed

In Jim Fisk's city, in debased New York ;

When it was further noised she carried on

With Loosealot, one of Guelpho's best-fed knights

Then he, believing this, feared lest his wife,

Imbibing these new doctrines from this Dame,

Should even more than heretofore demand

Her will and way ; nay more, perchance, maintain

Her right to flirt.   So, unto Guelpho going,

He made this pretext, that his tailor's bills,

The fearful price of coals, his debts at loo,

And all the varied costs of London life,

Demanded he should go to where his house

Rose desolate upon the Cornish coast.

Guelpho, who not a little loved Heraint,

Mused for a space upon his plea, but last

Allowing it, Heraint and Shenid rode

To where arose the station terminal

Of Paddington the Western ; and he, there

Taking two tickets for the down express,

Did, with his lady, pass to his own land.

Once there, Heraint grew yet more fond of her,

And compass'd her with sweet observances

And worship, never leaving her, and grew

Forgetful of his duties on the Bench,

Forgetful of his Yeoman cornetcy,

Forgetful of the partridge on the First,

Forgetful of the hound and of the hare.

And this forgetfulness was hateful to her ;

For all the country people when they met

In twos and threes, or fuller companies,

Began to scoff and jeer, and babble of him,

Saying the grey mare was the better horse,

And that she tied him to her apron-string.

So day by day she thought to tell Heraint

That, though she liked her way, she did not care

To have it yielded her so easily ;

That though she loved him, yet, in truth, she found

His constant presence bored her very much,

And, grateful as might be the country's joys,

She longed again for London and for life,

Full fain would mingle with the rush and rout,

And pass a season up in town once more.

At last it chanced that, on a summer's morn
(He'd had a heavy supper), the rude sun
Beat through the Helioscene into the room
And flashed in Heraint's yet unshaven face ;
Who, restless, cast the counterpane aside,
And kicked the clothes with passion purposeless.
Till Shenid woke and sat beside the bed
Half sleepily, and thought within herself,
Was ever man so imbecile as he ?
Was ever chin so raspy as is his ?
'Tis not a pleasant sight, and then she said,
Low to her own heart, peevishly she said :

" What makes him stay in this slow hole so long ?
Far liever would I tell my maid to pack
My travelling boxes, clamped with brazen nails,
And seek again our house in Curzon Street.
Can he be jealous ? Oh, the foolish man !
I'll make him jealous if we stay down here.
O me ! why don't he take me back to town ? "

Half-inwardly, half-audibly, she spoke,

And such her fretfulness it made her weep

Real tears, which, falling, chanced upon his nose,

And these awoke him, and it so turned out—

For so it suits the sequel of my song—

He heard some fragments of her later words.

How that she'd make him jealous, this he heard,

And how she longed with yearning for the town ;

And then he thought, "She loves me not ; she weeps

For some gay courtier in Guelpho's Court ;

She longs to leave our sweet Arcadian life ;

She tires of pasty and of fish profuse ;

She wearies of the welkin and the wave ;

O woe is me, she loves me not !" and so,

Burning with indignation, he assumed

A manner not his own ; and with a lurch

He rolled, and all but tumbled out of bed ;

Then, picking up himself, as does a man

Who, fallen, wishes to stand up again,

He rang the bell with violence, and cried,

" Bring Bradshaw and hot water ! " then to her—

" We will set out upon a trip to-day ;

So put you on some useful travelling-dress,

And come with me."   And Shenid asked, amazed,

" Whatever's up ? "   Then he, " Do as I say."

·And she aback quite taken by his tone,

Murmuritg, " My beauty, you shall pay for this,"

Did go and do, e'en as her loved had said ;

And op'ing wide a drawer, the bottom one,

Took out a French merino, claret-hued,

Unfolded it, and clothed herself therein,

Rememb'ring that in *that*, her only dress,

He learned to love her when they first had met,

When first he wooed her, as you now shall hear.

Heraint had once been travelling where the rails

Of iron, parallel, had not been laid.

A walking tour was his ; and late one night

He came, across a tarn, into a town

In a long valley, on one side whereof,

White from the plasterer's brush, a hostel rose,

And on one side a villa, semi-detached.

Going to the hostel—'twas the " Fox and Goose "—

He found it full, full to the stable-yard,

And asking why, one gruffly answered him,

" A man to-morrow morning's to be hanged ;

They've run cheap vans, and all the town is
    full."

So, hieing down the street, he found it so,

And listless wand'ring limpēd back again

To where the villa semi-detached uprose,

And saw in parlour-pane a card displayed,

Which spoke, in Roman type, of rooms to let.

So, thinking of a couplet dear to him,

Writ by a master-hand—he knew it well—

    " 'Tis better to have lodged and loved,

    Than never to have lodged at all,"

He pushed the gate, when came a maiden voice,

Which sang so sweetly that he straightway stopped,

And saw its owner—damsel fair was she—

And listened, while the song went on, and said.
" Here I at last have found the voice for me."

It chanced the song the maiden sang was one
Of Fortune and her wheel, and thus she sang :

" Turn, Fortune, turn thy wheel o'er Tiddler's
        grounds ;
Turn me a suitor with ten thousand pounds ;
    And then thy wheel and thee I will not hate.

" Turn, Fortune, turn thy wheel, but do not stay
Thy hand until a lover comes my way ;
    My hoard is little, but my wants are great ;

" Smile and I'll smile, scowl and I fain must frown
And if you throw me up, you'll cast me down ;
    For man is man and woman is his fate.

" Turn, turn thy wheel, and be it fast or slow,

O Fortune ! do not make your wheel my woe,

  Or I thy wheel and thee shall surely hate."

She ceased, and then Heraint went on and knocked,

And as the echo passed and died—I mean

Nothing anent the halfpenny sheet—there came

A girl ! from forehead down to toe-tip smeared

In kitchen messes, and in grease array'd,

Who, his soft speech anticipating, said,

" *The rooms is let !*" and would have slammed the

    door ;

But she who sang had seen the knight's approach,

Had eyed him from behind the parlour blind ;

Had seen with maid's keen glance he was a swell ;

So, hurrying out, did stop the servant naive,

And, smiling sweetly, said, " What can we do ? "

And he, all blushing, scraped upon the mat,

Saying, " I seek a harbourage for the night."

And she, " That means, I s'pose, you want a bed."

He nodded, then did follow her straight in

To where her father sat; and he, discreet,
Did note the crest on Heraint's *solitaires*,
And, knowing well *Debrett*, did smile on him
A hearty welcome to their frugal board;
For said the crafty Jones, Shenid's papa,
" We once were rich, now poor; the cause is near;
You see it in the line twelve miles from this,
That starts for nowhere, leads to nowhere, ends
But God knows where; it swallowed up my all.
Still we will make as merry as we may;
Stay you by all means, if you feel inclined."
He spoke, and from the buttery was brought
A wheaten loaf, a butter pat also;
Rare wines of household manufacture, too,
Rich gooseberry, ripe elder, graced the board;
Likewise a new-ope'd tin of sprat-sardines.
So then old Jones did say, " Fall to, O guest!
Make havoc with the fare upon the board."
And Heraint played him with a sham sardine,
Toyed with the cruet, dallied with his bread,—

As does the special of the *Telegraph*,—

And drank, from utter courtesy, some wine.

The supper passed, the gen'rous gooseberry warmed

His blood, and made him feel more amorous yet;

For Shenid was a winsome girl, and sweet

She was to look upon—more sweet to kiss.

Nodding, the father sat in distant chair,

Leaving his child and him to coo and court;

So much, that when the time had come for bed,

Heraint had longing in him then and there

To stoop and kiss the tender little thumb

That cross't the candlestick she gave to him;

And more, he, warm with wine, did kiss her lips,

As though he'd known her for a month of moons,

Which, battling prettily, she did permit,

And, catching her papa's old eye, did wink.

The morrow came, the man was hanged, and then

The tourists went their way, and all was peace.

But Heraint stayed and courted Shenid still,

And, last of all, did ask her to be his ;

To which, she being by nature not a fool,

Did make a slow yet sure response of " Yea."

So in due course he with the aged Jones

Was closeted ; and then in full quick time

Was joined to her in quite a quiet way.

She, maiden-like, had wished to cut a dash,

To go to church in carriages and pairs ;

With clanging bells, and favours white, and flowers,

With bridesmaids, bouquets, and in veil of lace,

To spite the girls she knew about the town ;

But he said " Nay," for he did not love fuss ;

" Keep on, my pet," said he, " that self-same dress

Which draped you when, all tired, you took me in."

So she, not liking yet to claim her way,

Kept on her French merino, claret-hued,

And, when the special licence had arrived,

In it by Holy Church was made a wife.

So now, that morning when he said to her,

" And you put on some useful travelling dress,"
She took this and array'd herself therein.

O purblind race of miserable men,
How many 'mongst us at this very hour
Do forge a life-long trouble for ourselves
By being o'er-suspicious !   We like trust—
As well our tailors know—but to the sex
We yield it not.   So 'twas with poor Heraint.

So made they for the station, where he took
Two first-class tickets for fair Exeter,
And then, because he loved her passionately,
And yet, poor silly soul, was jealous of her,
He took a corner seat, then said to her,
" Not at my side, nor opposite, but there,
I charge you sit as though you knew me not :
I charge you on your duty as a wife,
Whatever happens, not to speak a word.
No, not a word ! "   And Shenid was aghast,

Yet, murmuring still; " O ! you shall pay for this,"
She in the further corner meekly sat.

The train went forth, but scarce had 'gan to go,
When, crying out, " O, dullard that I am,
I have not got a paper," he his head
Put forth, and beckoned to a liveried youth,
Who, running, put the *Times* within his hand ;
And he exclaiming, " Hang the change ! my boy ! "
A shilling took and hurled it at his head.
So the last sight that Shenid had of home
Was that same boy with legs and arms all spread,
A diffuse cartwheel throwing in his glee.
Then—for the grinding brakes were now removed—
The snorting iron horse began to pant,
And his long tail of carriages to shake.
So on o'er fragile-fashioned viaducts,
And on through cuttings deep as sinners' doom,
By swamps and pools, waste places of the fen,
By wildernesses smelling of the sea,

D

By seaside towns—fell lodging harpies' holds—
By castles and by cottages they rode.
Round was their pace at first, but slackened soon,
What time his face behind his *Times* he hid;
While she, half frighten'd, still spoke never word,
But look'd on land and sea-scape listlessly;
Till the great screeching engine-whistle amazed
Her heart, and, glancing forth, she saw and heard
That they had reached fair Plymouth by its Sound.

Here a South Devon guard, broad-faced withal,
With under-fringe of beard of russet red,
The door wide opened—'twas on Shenid's side—
And cried with a big voice, " Your tickets, please ! "
But Heraint moved not, nor his paper moved.
She, helpless, for he held the tickets twain,
Looked wistfully, as looks the gutter-child
When, with nose flattened 'gainst the cook-shop
  pane,
It sees a party oleaginous

Cut out square blocks of steaming, fig-starr'd dough ;

But, mindful of his order, never spoke.

Then said the broad-faced one, "What, is he dead ?"

(He may, who knows ? have qualified the " he.")

So she, determining to brave his ire,

Sidled, like some sweet snake, along the seat,

Till, nearing him, she nudged his callous side,

Met his full frown, saucily firm, and said,

" Heraint, my dear Heraint, what, hear you not ?

Yon menial would our tickets duly punch."

He made a wrathful answer, " Did I ask

You what he wanted ? No, ma'am, I did not ;

I laid upon you not to speak to me ;

And thus you keep it. Well, then, look !" and then

With dexterous thumb and finger he drew out

The pasteboard passports from his sealskin pouch ;

Which taking, did the broad-faced menial punch,

And, grinning, passed away. Then he the two

Together putting, "Take them !" said to her,

" And keep them." And she put them in her purse.

At which time fain he would have spoken more,

And loosed in naughty words his smould'ring wrath ;

But ever more it seemed an easier thing

To fancy she was false than tell her so,

As doubtless many a married man has found

When he is jealous of his better half.

But why he acted with the tickets thus

The writer cannot say ; he cannot say.

But in a scarcely longer time than takes

An evening " print " to sell an edition out

Opened the door again, and one stepped in—

Full-chested, tawny-bearded, military,

If ever martial bearing stamped a man.

He, dropping in a seat—'twas facing hers—

At once made wicked lightnings of his eyes ;

Scarce had they started when to her he made

Meek offer of the *Graphic* and of *Punch*,

Asked was she going far ; she shook her head ;

And would she like the window down ; she frowned.

Heraint still hid his visage with the *Times*,

And Shenid knew not what to do or say,

Moved fretful in her seat with cheek aflame,

Looked long and often, but e'er looked in vain

Tow'rds where her husband sat ; and he, all stern,

Made never a sign, for 'twas his little game

To test her, as he thought.   Poor, silly man !

When now for many a mile the train had steamed,

The soot-grimed driver, looking far ahead,

Beneath his curved, rough hand, descried a speck,

Which, ever widening, was, he knew, " White-Ball "

(For thus the natives name the tunnel there).

Sounding his whistle then, he slackened speed,

And all the jolting train did screech and groan ;

Then with a crash like that of cataract,

Or city house which on a sudden " breaks,"

It rattled in, and all was densely dark.

Then he, the tawny-bearded one, put out

His wicked hand, and felt about for hers,

And in the darkness on her flaming cheek

She felt the soughing of his vicious breath,

Until he found her hand in kid-skin cased,

And would have squeezed it hard, perchance, but she,

Resenting it, sent forth a small, shrill scream,

As of a soft mouse taken in a trap,

Which sees a pussy glaring through the wires;

At which the amorous one drew back abashed.

But all too late, for in the murky gloom

An arm was waved, and then a big fist fell,

And 'fore the military's eyes danced sparks,

And, for the moment, he did feel all nose,

And, howling, took forthwith a secret vow

Never in tunnel more to try it on.

Then ceased the darkness, and into the day

The sinuous snake of locomotion passed.

And Heraint still was buried in his *Times;*

Shenid gazed straight into the flying fields;

While he, the tawny one, was lost in *Punch,*

And in a handkerchief with gore besmirched.

And when the train next into stillness stole
He took his hat, passed out, and seeking, found
Another carriage, and no more was seen.

But when the fourth part of the day was done
They by the foreshores of the Exe had passed,
And, 'lighting on the platform with her lord,
Then Shenid knew that Exeter was gained.
Up through the quaint old streets they went, until
A hostelry ecclesiastical,
That might have been an abbot's dwelling-place,
With gothic windows, doors of gnarlēd oak,
Rose on their right, at which the fly did stop.
Three steps of stone led to a spacious hall,
On which ope'd doors on every side, and one,
Which bore the legend " Coffee Room " upon it,
Did they pass through, and Heraint rang the bell.
Then came a weak-kneed waiter, pasty-faced,
His manner meek, his footstep plantigrade,
With " Yes, sir," brimming on his treacherous lips ;

And, flicking at a crumb imaginary

With napkin which he wore upon his arm,

Did stand, and list while Heraint told his wants,

And how he would of wine, and meat, and bread,

Which having called for, he, considerate still,

Though silent to her ever, furthermore

Said, " Waiter, bid to come the chambermaid,

To show this lady to a sleeping-room."

So Shenid went, and, all amazed to find

How strict her lord kept to his strange resolve,

Did dress her hair with more than common care,

And used her most effective toilette tricks ;

Then, pouting prettily, and muttering " Plums,"

She, with a noiseless step, did gain the stairs.

But ere she reached the sixth—there were eighteen—

She was aware of voices down below,

And, looking, saw behind a half-shut door

Three figures standing ; one the waiter was,

And one the landlord, and the third his wife.

And Shenid heard the wicked landlord say,

" You're sure you rightly saw our victim's name ? "

To him the waiter, " Yes, it's on the trunks."

And great glee mantled in the landlord's face.

" My dear," he said, " 'tis well ; the name I know

As that of one whom we may safely fleece,

Who has much money and but little wit,

Who'll pay without a murmur or a word.

 Tis well indeed ; bring forth for him and his

The home-made port we charge fifteen-and-six ;

Prepare for him the stuffy sitting-room

Whose rental is a guinea for a day ;

Charge waxen candles by the pound, and put

Etceteras in his bill with lavish pen ;

Let every mouthful of the food he eats

Be booked as though he had a golden meal.

Come, let us fleece him right and left, my wife ! "

And she, agreeing, kissed her lord for joy.

Then Shenid ponder'd in her heart, and said,

" I will go down and tell this to Heraint.

I'll tell him all the caitiff landlord's talk,

And warn him of the port, and tell him not
To light a candle even when 'tis dusk;
For though he's told me not to dare to speak,
I can't be silent while this wicked pair
Take money from him that may p'rhaps be mine."
So slipped she down all noiselessly, and found
Her liege lord where she left him, and she said,
" Heraint, I saw three bandits in the bar
Plotting your pillage, and I heard them boast
That they would fleece you, and possess your purse—
Would make you pay for candles by the pound,
Decant you home-made port and charge the same
An awful price per bottle, and, indeed,
Would rob you in all ways conceivable."

To which he flung a wrathful answer back,
For he was hungry, " What is this you say ?
I told you not speak to me at all.
'Tis nonsense, let them do their worst; for I
Have travelled in the Highlands, and have felt

What Gaelic landlords in the season do—
An ordeal this that fits me for the worst
That West of England landlords may essay."
Then ceased, but pond'ring over Shenid's words,
Remembered she had said the coming port
Was of home manufacture ; and this thought,
When dwelt on, proved too much for him, and so,
Speaking again, he said, " Put on your things,
And you shall see my vigour is not lost."

Then Shenid dressed, and waited on the stairs,
And Heraint came to beard the bandits three ;
What time the landlord with a nimble pen
Made out and added up prospective bills,
While deft his wife poured out the log-wood broth,
And while the waiter dreamed of lavish " tips."
They, looking up, observed him, and the last
Said, " Coming, sir " ; but Heraint bid him go,
And, turning to the host, he crossly cried,
"Thy reckoning, man !" and, ere he learnt it, "Take

This sov'reign!" and he therewith flung one down.

And, all amazed, the hostess and the host,

With much concern, asked wherefore and for why

The Lord Heraint thus acted; and with scorn

He pointed to the British port, and said,

"O villain, well thou know'st why I am going;

It's no light thing to sell such stuff as that,

Not fit for eleemosynary spread,

Not worthy of a Putney publichouse.

Have thou a care; I'll tell thy shameless crime

To all I meet; I'll put it in the *Times,*

And thy hotel shall be a byword, there!"

Then he to Shenid, "Forward!" and they went

With maledictions as they crossed the mat.

And, hungry still, Heraint did seek a shop

Where hams in cut and salted beef were rife,

And, sending out for Bass's Bitter Beer,

They lunched right well and yet right frugally;

Which done, again the twain set forth to walk

In silence, and the station reached, where he
Again took tickets two, this time for town,
And when the train came—not before—got in.

Then forward by a way—a six-foot way,
Which travellers by the rail all know so well—
And she looked out at one side, he the same
Did at the other, till, with luckless aim,
A cinder from the engine met his eye,
And sent him in to rub it and to moan.
But on they went at forty miles per hour,
Flashed by the white poles of the telegraph,
Clattered through cuttings, hedges hurried by,
Raced silly cows, and frightened nervous sheep ;
Ploughed through the pleasaunces of Taunton Dean,
Shot by Bridgewater, redolent of bricks,
And Weston-super-Mare in the mud ;
Till, as the hours chased on, was Bristol reached,
And Bath, where bubbles up the igneous spring ;
And, stern in purpose, Heraint all the while

Had sacredly behind his paper kept ;

And many passengers came in and went,

But he went reading on and on for ever,

Until he could from iterated gaze

Recount its all and every content ;

Had scanned the Births, and Marriages and Deaths,

The column read where agony is piled,

Perused the " leaders," skipped the telegrams,

Wondered who 'twas that read the Shipping News,

Noted the comments meteorological,

And searched the advertising columns well,

Seeing with jealous eye and longing heart,

" Connubial Bliss " announced, price but twelve-
       pence.

But still he would not speak to her, and she

Grew 'customed to his mood, it heeded not,

Looked out and in, read, ate, worked, yawned and
       slept,

And marvelled how much longer 'twas to last.

On a sudden, when they scarce had well got through

The lengthened bore at Box that's situate,

Another screech, another scrunch, and, lo !

Another stoppage spoke of Swindon reached.

Down dropped the *Times*, and, striding quickly out,

Heraint in silence helped fair Shenid down,

And motioning to her to seek the door

Where " first-class " customers were waited on,

Himself sought moodily the " second-class."

Hardly her door—it was a swinging one,

Pushed from without—was driven back to the wall,

When, midmost of a rout of passengers

Crumpled, and hot, and dissolutely pale,

Her suitor in old days before Heraint,

Entered, the pert and penniless De Bauch.

He, moving up with pliant courtliness,

Saw Shenid, with the corner of his eye,

Sitting alone, all solitary sad,

Looking upon the waiting South Wales train,

And knew her.   Then he cried for goodly cheer,

For segments of pork-pies, for sandwiches,

For cake of Banbury, and for bun of Bath,

For sherry of—well, who can tell of where ?—

To feed his sudden guest, and, going up,

Presented them with humbleness to her.

Then, while she trifled with a piece of pie—

For she had recognised him—he sat down

Close by her side, and uttered, whisperingly :

" Shenid, my early and my only love !

(He had five sweethearts at that very time.)

Shenid, where have you been for all these months ?

How we have missed you up in town this year !

What chance is this ?   How is it I see you here ?

Are you alone ?   And, tell me, where is he—

The man who is to you what I should be ?

You come with no attendance, page or maid,

To serve you—does he love you as of yore ?

If so, why this merino, worn and old ?

You do not love him now ; I see it all.

You tire of him, and he, p'rhaps, tires of you,

And you were coming up to town, to me—

To me who love you as I did before.

For have you not a fortune now, my own ?

Say, do you love me, Shenid, say, O say !

Come, fly with me; there waits the South Wales
    train ;

Your word, your purse, and I will tickets take,

For Glo'ster, Chelt'nham, Cardiff, anywhere—

Come, only say you're mine, for ever mine."

But she, still toying with her pie, cast down

Her eyes as though she would observe with care

Its parts component and concomitant.

Then, when in earnestness his eyes were cast

Down to her feet—'tis meet to say just here

All else were far too hungry to remark

This little episode of Swindon love—

She, having taken up some crumbs of bread,

Had rolled them in a pellet round and hard,

And catching, through a vista of men's heads,

Of barmaids' hair, of urns, and evergreens,

A sight of her lord's head, far, far away,

And of his face, or all of it, in sooth,

By rim of pewter flagon uneclipsed,

Rose up and aimed with all her woman's might

The wheaten bullet at her husband's head,

Which, glancing from a bagman's tall white hat,

Made havoc 'mongst some pickles 'neath his nose.

Amazed, and angry, did Heraint look up,

Saw, then, her hand that hurled, and caught her
    eye,

Which said as plain as human eye can say—

And oh! what tales these visual organs tell—

" Put down your beer, and come here, quick ; I want
    you ! "

So, hurrying round —for how could he resist,

His heart being warmed with sausages and stout ?—

He broke upon her hastily, and said,

" What is it now—another broad-faced guard ? "

But she, with look contemptuous, pointed at

The base De Bauch, who sat close by her side.

And then she said, " Have I your leave to speak ? "

And he, " You take it, speaking."   And she spoke,

Much to the barmaids' and the others' glee.

" This man, Heraint," she said, " has thought it well

To come to me with pie and protestations,

To pair devotion off with Banbury cake,

To woo me, as he thought, with buns of Bath.

But I despise him.   Have at him, good lord ! "

And Heraint would, no doubt, have had at him,

Have brained him with a bottle, spoil'd his face

With boiling tea, or choked him with a cork,

But at that moment rang the second bell,

And all going on, their seats for London took.

Not quite convinced, though well-nigh so, Heraint

Once more put up his *Times*, but soon it fell,

And nid, nid, nodding, soon he seemed to sleep.

She then came closer to him, mighty pleased—

His hasty meal had done no harm to him,—

And hung above him, listening to his breath,

Till, with a woman's craft, she knew he shammed.

Then, taking off her hat and out her pins,

She let her hair fall in a golden shower,

And, putting up her hands, began to tear

It delicately, saying, as she did—

" O woe is me! for I have grieved my lord:

O woe is me! he will not let me speak.

Yet how I love him—him and none beside—

So much (how deep she was) that I would take,

If he would come with me, two tickets back

To where his Cornish mansion rears itself,

And never, never say again 'twas dull."

Then, with an effort—'twas a desp'rate one—

She squeezed three warm, round tears upon his face.

Yet he lay still, and feigned himself asleep,

That he might prove her to the uttermost,

And say to his weak heart, " She weeps for me."

But when for very titillation he

Could no more keep his slumber so well feigned,

He, rousing up, did pluck her by the hand,

And, saying "I have done you wrong, Shenid,"

Did kiss her, and she knew her turn was come,

So waited patiently, and heard him say,

"Henceforward I will rather die than doubt;

And here I promise never more shall pass

A season but we will be up in town,

And bonnets shall be yours at your sweet will,

And jewels, and dresses, and all else *galore*."

So Shenid chuckled inwardly, and said

This to herself: "I've done a good day's work;

He's more than ever in my power.   O fool,

To think that he could get the better o' me!"

So, getting out at Paddington, where, warned

By lightning-wire, a carriage waited them,

They entered, passed to Curzon Street, Mayfair,

And for a tale of months did there rèside.

While there, space fails to tell the merry tale

Of all the routs, and balls, and dinners given,

Of all the gorgeous dresses Shenid wore,

Of all the compliments she did receive—

Or nasty speeches when her back was turned.

Guelpho was glad to have Lord Heraint back,

And cast royal sheep's-eyes at his pretty wife,

And chaffed her husband for his " spooniness."

But he—the husband—never doubted more,

But rèsted in her fealty, until

A fit of gout, hereditary, came,

And, flying to his stomach, took him home.

Then Shenid, still most comely, wed again,

And when the second died, yet once again.

Then also she gave in, and was at peace.

VILIEN.

VILIEN.

HERLIN, the Wizard Herlin, was a man
Of wondrous powers, deep skilled in magic lore,
Learned in legerdemain, a conjurer
Of no mean order, and, forsooth, well-known
As an accomplished prestidigitateur.
Oft had he figured at the Egyptian Hall,
By flaming posters on the walls announced ;
Oft had he in the drawing-room appeared,
And charmed and awed with necromantic arts.
Such were his gifts it fails to here set forth
The talents various of that mystic man.
Not only could he emulate the acts
Of him whom men call Wizard of the North ;
Not only could he play strange tricks with cards,
Bring bowls of golden fish from 'neath his coat,

Produce a thousand toys from one small hat,

And from one bottle draw a dozen drinks ;

He, more, possessed the gift of second sight,

Out-faked the Fakir of Oloolulu

In his peculiar mesmeric deeds,

And beat the best known of Biologists.

For table-turning he possessed a gift ;

Could raise up spirits quite as readily

As some men put them down.   Moreover, he

Knew all the tricks of Pepper and of Dirck ;

Had been to Mrs. Guppy's on a time,

And at Southampton Row had played his part ;—

In short his magic powers were manifold.

He, the most famous wizard of the day,

Who had 'fore many crowned heads performed,

Including, chiefly, those who ruled no more

But linger'd then upon a foreign strand,

Had come in time to be remarked at Court,

And to be asked for by the coming K——,

Who, hearing his renown, sent equerries
To bid him to the palace ; and he came.

Once there, he showed to Guelpho all his art,
His rarest tricks, his most mysterious feats ;
Turned oranges to eggs, took handkerchiefs,
Which, to all semblance burned, he yet restored
All whole ; fired pistol-shots, did he,
At Guelpho's hat, and then found 'neath it birds.
A table—ebon was it, and inlaid
With yellow ivory from the Eastern East—
He made to rap the Coming K——'s right age—
'Twas right to one year by the almanacks—
And then it spelt the name of one he loved ;
At which the knights all bowed in merry mirth,
But Cuelpho blushed, and felt him ill at ease,
And mused, "What power is this I feel and see ?"
So, when again the tell-tale table rapped
This time another name beloved by him,
He, all ablaze, went rushing from the room,

And Herlin packed up all his traps and " sloped."

But came upon the Coming K—— next day

A fresh desire to see the magic man ;

For, seeing him, he thought, perchance I may

His art discover and his problems solve.

So came he with a budget of fresh tricks,

And did new feats with clever sleight of hand ;

Found money flying in the atmosphere ;

Took lemons out from where *was* Guelpho's hair,

And rabbits from a high-born lady's lap ;

The ebon table brought again, and did

Fresh myst'ries with it, yet more wonderful ;

At which the Coming K—— did blankly gaze.

For, mused he, if the table tells my age,

And whom I love, and raps their cherished names,

Why should it not yet more and more reveal,

Foretell my future, and lay bare my life ?

(How knew he Schneider, and large-eyed Judic ?)

Then, roused to action, he to Herlin went,

And said, " The secret of your table tell,

And you shall be a Dinner-Table Knight ;

Shall be my guide, and counsellor, and friend :

No candle to you shall a ' comique ' hold."

But Herlin thought a space, then reverently

Placed on his nose's side his finger first,

And tapped it twice : and Guelpho knew the sign.

There was, it happ'd, just then about the Court

A maid of waiting on the *Gallic fay*,

Called Vilien ; wily she was and fair,

An arrant flirt as e'er used Persian Bloom.

In gay Lutætia she had won her spurs,

A favoured guest of him who lost Sedan.

She had seen Herlin's magic, and his arts.

He, too, had lit upon her with his eyes,

And looked to love, for she was very sweet.

And he—well he was foreign, and not rich,—

So he had used his wizard's power to bring

Her close to him, and had her by his side

To hold out hats ; to mark the half-a-crowns ;

To choose the cards, and fire the pistol off;
Had borrowed her lace handkerchief—indeed,
Much service had she rendered unto him;
While she, all ready for a little fun,
With count or conjurer, 'twas all the same,
Had let him squeeze her hand, and even once
A kiss snatch from her just behind his screen.
This maiden, then, it so turned out, next day
To that on which was Guelpho so perplexed,
Had met him walking grumpily along,
And would have wrought upon his cloudy mood
With saucy eyes, mock-loyal, and pitying voice,
And flattered adoration; and she said,
" What ails my lord the Coming K—— to-day?"
And Guelpho told to her his mournful tale;
How he would fain himself a table own
Which could inform him of what was to be—
Forgetful of the fact that Herlin did
But tell him of what had already been.
" I want the secret of this magic man!"

Cried Guelpho, "that I may the secret use."

And Vilien answered, "Leave it all to me ;

I will obtain it. Trust me, that will I."

So saying, leapt impetuous on her way,

Leaving the Coming K—— in wonderment.

It took but minutes few for her to gain

The Egyptian Hall, for there she thought to see

The Wizard Herlin, but instead she saw

A placard posted on the door which said,

In scarlet letters on a dirty ground,

" The Wizard Herlin's on his country tour,

And will reopen here in Christmas week."

"Foiled ! foiled !" cried Vilien, in so loud a tone,

That neighbouring cab steeds reared upon the rank.

But, heedless, she gained Burlington Arcade,

And there determined on her future plans,

First buying of a boy a *Telegraph*.

Not far had she its pristine page perused

Ere some such words as follow met her eye :

" The Wizard Herlin begs to here announce

His autumn tour.   To-morrow he will be
At Weston-super-Mare, for three days ;
Friday, Bridgewater; Taunton, Monday next."
And that was all.   Yet beamed fair Vilien's face,
And twinkled both her eyes triumphantly.
" 'Tis well," she muttered as she tripped away.
" She's daft," the Beadle cried, and so she passed.

Sped four glad days, and down Bridgewater's streets
A two-horse 'bus went rattling ; and inside
Sat Vilien, comely in her glee ; the 'bus
Stopt with a sudden jerk before the hotel,
And, picking up her traps, stept Vilien out.
The landlord came with polished courtesy,
And bade her welcome, and her room prepared.
But, restless ever, Vilien fumed and fussed ;
Till, finding speech, she uttered words like these,
"I think, good host," (pray note she said "Good
     host ")
"A wizard is at present in your town ? "

" In sooth, fair lady," did the host reply,

" There's one announced to show this very night

His tricks and strange illusions at our hall."

" His name ?" gasped Vilien, clinging to a chair.

" Is Herlin," quoth the landlord, turning pale.

" Enough," she cried ; " go send your ' Boots ' at
    once,

And book for me the very foremost place ;

If needs be, book me several ! " and he went.

The evening came, and at the Town Hall doors

A crowd of three stood all incontinent,

And one was Vilien.   And when the bolt,

By hidden hand withdrawn, went shooting back,

The three rushed in, and Vilien first of all.

A dim, sad light burned in the Borough Hall,

For gas was six and six per thousand feet,

And on the platform at the farther end

The magic apparatus was arranged.

There was the table gilded, bound with fringe,

F

With hollow legs, and nests of secret-drawers ;
There was the cage in which the doves are found ;
The pack of cards, the saucer, and the plates ;
The boxes too, false-bottomed every one ;
The nest of funnels, and the usual eggs ;
Behind all which a curtain hung in folds,
Embroidered with the zodiacal signs ;
And at the sight a hush fell on the three,
And one—a young boy—muttered o'er his prayers.

So silence reigned ; and as it reigned there came
A few fresh people into the back seats.
But Vilien sat, and presently she saw
A face appear between the mystic folds,
And knew it by the token to be his !—
His, Herlin's, his she came to seek—
And chuckled audibly ; and Herlin heard,
And saw her face, and wondered at the sight,
Then disappeared, and all again was still,
Till, with a creak, beside the platform oped

A little door, and from it came a hand
Which beckoned Vilien ; and the maiden went,
E'en to the little room behind the stage
In which the wizard had his tricks prepared.

Once there, the wizard placed a chair, and said,
" How, maiden, is it that I see you here ? "
And she, dissembling, turned her treacherous eyes
Upon his face, and said, " How can you ask ? "
There sat she on that chair—a dusty one—
As if in deepest reverence and in love ;
While Herlin, with a sweet apology,
Continued to prepare his magic art,
And, moving carelessly, trod on her toe.
At which she winced, and cried out, " Trample me !
Big foot, that I have followed down from town,
And I will pay you worship ; tread me down,
And I will bless you for it."   He was mute,
And many thoughts went rolling through his brain,
As in the season many hansom cabs

Go wildering on down Piccadilly steep.
So, when she lifted up her face and said,
" O, did you mean to do it ? " and again,
" O, did you mean to do it ? " and once more
" O, did you mean to do it ? " he was mute.
And pretty Vilien, lifting up her gown,
Shuffled her chair quite closely unto him ;
Catching his hand in hers, her other arm
She curved around his neck, and with its hand
Caught the long end of his be-waxed moustache,
And pulled it hard.   And then he spoke and said,
" I really beg your pardon."   Vilien smiled,
Let go his tortured hirsute ornament ;
And so the wizard did his task pursue,
While she exclaimed, with saucy, pleasing smile,
" What, O my wizard ! have you found your voice ?
I bid the stranger welcome.   Thanks at last."

And Herlin took her hand in his, and said,
" You do not tell me why it is you're here ;

To what I owe your pretty patronage.
Five days ago I left the Egyptian Hall,
Because, forsooth, I could not make it pay,
And came down here ; you followed me unask'd,
And when I looked and saw you in the hall
I felt at first annoyed.　To tell the truth,
I feared you would with business interfere,
And sweep me from my hold upon the world,
And spoil my name and fame.　Your pardon, miss,
But just now have I no time left to flirt ;
So say your will ; explain what 'tis you want,
And go, for it is close on eight o'clock."

And Vilien answered, smiling mournfully :
" I ever fear'd you were not wholly mine.
And see—you ask me what it is I want.
Yet people call you wizard—why is this ?
What is it makes you seem so proud and cold ?
Yet if you'd really know what boon I ask,
Then tell me, dearest Herlin, ere I go,

The charm with which you make your table rap
What passes of the waving hand it needs
To make it tilt upon its ebon legs,
And rap out secrets to the listening world.
'Tis this I want to know; this must I know
As proof of trust. O Herlin, tell it me.
The charm thus told will satisfy me quite,
And I will leave you to perform your art;
Will ever look on you as truest friend.
How hard you look, and how denyingly!
O, if you think this wickedness in me
That I should tell the secret to the world
To make you lose your well-earned name and fame;
That makes me fit to cry. O, yield my boon,
And grant my re-reiterated wish;
Then will I love you, ay. and you shall kiss
My grateful lips—you shall upon my word."

And Herlin took his hand from hers and said,
" O, Vilien, ask not this, but aught beside.

Wouldst know the bottle-trick ?   I'll tell it thee.
The magic candles ?   Them will I explain.
Ask of me how I shoot the pistol off,
And find the ladies' rings in flower-pot hid,
And thou shalt know it all.   Or wouldst thou learn
The way to fill a hat with divers sorts
Of bonbons, worsted balls, and penny toys ?
That, too, thou shalt be told.   All tricks with cards
I'll make to thy sweet comprehension plain ;
E'en my most famous globe of gold-fish trick
I'll make as simple as an A, B, C.
But as thou lov'st me, Vilien, do not ask
The way in which I make the table rap.
O ask it not ! "   And Herlin groaned, and smashed
A plate of eggs in his extreme dismay.

And Vilien, like the tenderest-hearted maid
That ever jilted swain or lover mocked,
Made answer, either eyelid wet with tears :
" Nay, Herlin, if you love me say not so ;

You do but tease to talk to me like this.
Methinks you hardly know the tender rhyme
Of 'Trust me for all in all or not at all.'
I heard a ' comique ' sing the verses once,
And they shall answer for me.   List the song :

' In love, 'tis as in trade ; if trade were ours,
  Credit and cash could ne'er be equal powers :
    Give trust to all or don't give trust at all.

' It is the little rift within the lute
  That cracks the sound and makes the music
      mute,
  And leaves the banjo nothing worth at all.

' It is the little moth within the suit,
  It is the merry maggot in the fruit,
    That worming surely, slowly ruins all.

' It is the little leaven makes the lump,

It is the little piston works the pump ;
   And A-L-L spells ALL, and all is all.'

O, Herlin, do you understand my rhyme ? ''

And Herlin coughed and owned that he did not ;
Yet did he half believe her to be true,
So tender was her voice, so fair her face,
So sweetly gleam'd her eyes with spurious tears ;
Just as the disinfected shrimp looks red,
And passes off as fresh though he is stale.
Still, though, he answered, half indignantly —
'' I cannot tell the meaning of your song ;
My time is precious ; come, young woman, hence ! ''

And Vilien, naught abashed, replied again :
'' Lo, now, how silly you must be, you know,
My simple stanzas not to understand ;
'Tis thus our truest poets write their rhymes :
They try their sense and meaning to conceal ;

But you should solve their riddles, though 'tis said
They don't the answers know themselves, sometimes.
However, be that as it may, I think
I'll give you one verse more." So Vilien sang .

" ' That sign, once mine, is thine, ay, closelier mine,
   For what is thine is mine, and mine is thine,
   And this, I much opine, is line on line ;
   So learn the obvious moral once for all.' "

But Herlin looked aghast, as well he might,
Nor knew the teaching of her little song.
Yet did he not the table-secret tell,
But this he told her ; 'twas, he said to her,
A story as in guerdon for her rhyme.

" There lives a man, not older much than I,
Who knows the table-trick three times as well ;
It has to him brought name, and fame, and gold.
He now is held in reverence for his art ;

For he can do strange tricks, to which compared,

The table-rapping business sinks to naught.

Seek out that man, he's probably at home,

And he will tell you far more wondrous things;

Will teach you how to float high in the air,

To walk upon the ceiling like a fly;

To elongate yourself a foot or two;

To pass yourself through close-locked doors: to
draw

Berlin wool patterns by the spirits' aid;

To summon ghosts up from the vasty deep;

And many such all-weird and occult things.

'Twas he taught me the trick; he'll tell it you;

So go and leave me, for my hour is nigh."

But Vilien put her lithe arm round his neck,

And stroked his cheeks, and played with both his
ears.

"Why trouble me to seek that man?" she said.

"You know the trick, and you must tell it me.

O crueller than ever told in tale,
Or sung in song!   O vainly cruel man!
You must the secret tell me ere I go."

She paused, and from the hall outside there came
The sound of stamping feet and clapping hands,
And noise as if some big umbrella sticks
Had been brought down with force upon the floor.
Which hearing, Herlin to the curtain stepped,
And, drawing it, looked out, and this he saw:
The stalls contained six people, three of whom
Had come with orders from the local prints;
One was the landlord of the Ship Hotel,
At which the wizard stayed; he came in free;
The two remaining ones had, weakly, paid.
The shilling seats contained about a score,
And in the back ones mustered twice that tale;
Though these included many who'd not paid,
Such as the billsticker and all his brats,
Policemen not on duty, and the crier.

Though few the audience, great the noise they made,
Especially the ones who came in free,
For it was eight o'clock, and at that hour
The bills announced the wizard would commence.
The uproar still increased ; the local press
Did to a man begin to hoot and howl.
The billsticker—his bill was yet unpaid—
Hammered his hob-nailed boots with savage force,
And all the back seats clapped their hands and
    yelled,
And Herlin trembled, and his face turned pale.

The money-taker came with one, twelve, six ;
'Twas all the coin he'd taken at the door ;
And said to Herlin, " You had best commence."
But, ah ! that money-taker knew not all ;
For just outside the door of Herlin's room
There stood the grim custodian of the Hall,
Who would have guineas three, the evening's rent,
Before he'd let the conjurer begin.

No wonder as the noise outside increased
That Herlin trembled and his face grew pale,
For save the one, twelve, six he'd just received,
He had but three-and-sixpence in the world.
" See, Vilien ! " he cried, " my doleful plight,
Nor vex me with thy vain request again ;
I am a ruined wizard, for the mob
Will all demand their money back, and then
My name and fame are gone.   Oh ! woe is me !
You haven't, I suppose, a pound or two
Loose change about you, have you, Vilien dear ? "

Then Vilien answered, " No ; but if you tell
The thing I ask, I'll see what I can do."
" By all means see," he said ; and so she saw.
But while she hasted back to her hotel
To fetch some coinage from her travelling-bag,
The storm increased, and there arose a cry
" Where is the wizard ? " and the wizard winced.
And then the billsticker, who smelt a rat,

And trembled for the sum of his account,
Said, " I'll be paid, at any rate," and hied
And came him to the little inner room
Where sat the conjurer, and said, " Look yere!
I want my seven-and-six," and had it too.
For he was fierce and strong, and Herlin funked.
What time the uproar in the front increased,
And there were shouts to have their money back,
Especially from those who had not paid.
And one there flung a chair upon the stage,
Which falling on, demolished, all the glass
Spread on the tables.   Thus did chaos come.
The wizard, fearing for his limbs, looked out,
And saw his apparatus all destroyed,
And moaning, " Thou art all too late, too late
To save me, Vilien!" made resolve to fly,
And fled, eluding the sharp gaze and grasp
Of him who kept the hall in custody ;
But, passing out into the street, it chanced
That he was by the cruel billposter seen,

Who, rushing in the hall, gave the alarm,
And all the audience hurried out in chase.

With rapid stride the baffled wizard flew,
With three times twenty at his glancing heels.
His pale blood, as he got up steam and ran,
Took gayer colours, like an opal warm'd.
And fast he ran ; and ever in his rear
Bellowed the " poster " and the following crowd.
His eyes began to start from out his head,
Till by a happy instinct he took out
The one pound five that still to him remained,
And flung it headlong at the coming crew.
It glittered in the light, and fell with chink
Upon the road.   At once it stopped pursuit ;
And while they scrambled for it in the street,
He fell in Vilien's arms, and was at peace.

Then in one moment she put in his hands
Three pounds and Guelpho's cheque for fifteen more :

A sum for which the wizard would have sold
His mother, had a buyer her desired.
" Tell me the charm," she cried.   He, panting,
    said,
" It all depends upon the wrist ; if that
Is strong, with practice you will quickly make
The heaviest table tilt on end and rap.
As to the rest—it's humbug all of it,
And it will rap just what you make it rap."
" That all !" she cried ; and he, " Oh yes, that's
    all ! "
And put the eighteen pounds into his purse.
Then she exclaimed, " I think I have been sold ; "
And shrieking out " O, fool !" the maiden leapt
Into the 'bus, and reached the station in't ;
Then, taking one for London—single, first—
She passed away, still muttering " O, fool ! "
But he, with eighteen pounds in hand, lay hid
For half a day, then passed he too, and found
Appreciation for his magic art

In Australasia and the Southern Seas.

While Guelpho never looks at Vilien now

But what he thinks of how they two were sold,

And how the wizard proved too much for them.

LOOSEALOT AND DELAINE.

LOOSEALOT AND DELAINE.

DELAINE the fair, Delaine the flirty one,
Delaine the arch-coquette of Clapham Rise,
Safe in her bed-room on the first floor front
Guarded the relics of her Loosealot,
Especially a large umbrella, green,
And battered by the storms of many months;
His letters too, and floral offerings,—
Within a secret-drawer of her desk,
Scented with fragrant patchouli they lay.
And scarce a day but she would take them out,
And read the letters through most carefully,
And ponder much for one so young and fair.

How came this maiden by these proofs of love
Of Loosealot's—she that knew not ev'n his name—
For he, with cunning deep, had signed it Smith ?

'Twas thus : he met her when he rode to shoot
In Hurlingham's great tournament of doves,
Which Guelpho had ordained, and which was held
In reverence by the doughtiest of his knights

For Guelpho, ere his was a crownèd head,
Roving the brick-curst realms of Shepherd's Bush,.
Dropped on a meadow hemmed about with trees,
With park, and garden, and a house behind ;
And, taking counsel with his chiefest chums,
With Northerland, surnamed the King of Fire,
With Coachington the horsey, and the rest,
They hit upon a new and chivalrous sport,
Well worthy of their prowess and their pride.
The tilt and tourney had grown flat and stale ;
Save surgeons, none now used the trusty lance,
And fencing was but practised verbally ;
So came it to their hardy souls to plan
Another sport befitting Englishmen,
Some dangerous game to try their British pluck,

Some noble trial to test their British strength ;

And presently these valiant ones conceived

A timid pigeon fastened in a trap,

At which, when loosened, they might stand and
    shoot,

Was sport well suited for strong men like them,

And worthy of young hardy Englishmen ;

And so these shooting matches came to be.

'Twas late in June, and it had been announced

That for the challenge cup the trial was fixed.

The Coming K—— had said he would be there,

And all his Carpet Knights had like intent,

Save Loosealot, and he was not in town,

Which much grieved Guelpho.   But there was a cause

Why Loosealot showed not up in town just then.

'Twas all about a mare called Goanveer ;

But what it was it needs not now to say,

Save that this mare was " dark " and was to run

In Guelpho's colours for the Riband Blue.

But Loosealot, where he was—it boots not where—
Heard of the coming shooting for the cup,
And, being a crack shot, liked it not at all
That he should miss the chance of winning it.
True, he was loth to leave sweet Goanveer ;
But then he too was loth to lose the cup.
So, fearing Guelpho's ire, he thus resolved
That he would go to Hurlingham *incog.*,
And shoot as one of that large family
Which glories in the sounding name of Smith ;
So, taking all precaution, and his gun,
Left Goanveer and hied for Hurlingham.
Alas! though, as it chanced, that direful day,
The train, through signals unpropitious,
Collided with a row of cattle trucks,
And, close to Clapham Junction, came to grief.
Well shaken, but unhurt, did Loosealot leap
From out the carriage-window, looked around,
And, seeing progress was not probable
By rail, took to his feet and lost his way,

Till, as on Clapham Common fell the night,
And o'er Tulse Hill the twinkling stars looked down,
He came upon a pathway in the waste,
And haply stumbled on a house or two.
The first he reached he stopped at, gave a knock,
And also rang ('twas writ up " Ring also "),
And brought a staid domestic to the door.
" Could you," said Loosealot, in knightly tones,
" Tell me the nearest way to Hurlingham ?
Or where there is a cab-stand or a 'bus,
Or if the gliding tram-cars pass this way ? "
The myriad-wrinkled woman stood and paused,
Then said, " Of 'Urlingham I never 'eard ;
But you can get a 'bus down at the ' Plough ' ;
Or there's a cab-stand in the Clap'am Road."
Just then came up the front steps two young men,
Who had but lately left their city haunt ;
These, seeing Loosealot, knew him for a swell,
Said to him, " Step you in, and we will see
How best you may attain to your desire."

So Loosealot, tired and faint, stepped gladly in,
And found inside the master of the house,
Who, bowing, bade him welcome ; and anon,
A maid came in, and this maid was Delaine,
Who, seeing there was company, did feign
She had not known it, and was running back,
When Loosealot, gallant, spite his horseyness,
Made protest, and the maiden did return.
" This is Delaine," her Pa said to his guest,
" And you are——?" Here he waited for the name.
" Smith," said the crafty Loosealot—" Sir Smith ;
You may, perchance, have heard the name before ;
I'm bound for Hurlingham, where, as you know,
There's soon to be a tournament of doves ;
'Tis late to-night, and if you have a bed
To spare, why I shall be obliged to you."

Then said Delaine's Papa (his name was Brown),
" Most certainly ; my son Sam's you can have,
For he can sleep for once with Nicholas ;

His ye can have." Then added his son Sam,
" Yea, take my bed by all means." Then Delaine
Looked archly up, and Loosealot met her eye,
And cried, " 'Tis settled, then ; I'll stay all night."

So this being thus (Sam did for him turn out),
They all began to talk of divers things.
" What is the prize for which you shoot ? " asked
Sam.
" A massive silver cup," said Loosealot.
" I'd like to have a try," said Nicholas.
" You cannot shoot, you silly," said Delaine.
But Loosealot chiefly looked at her fair face,
And worked his chair round nearer unto hers,
And whispered, " Should I this grand trophy win,
I wonder if Miss Brown would it accept ? "
Then flushed Delaine—it was a trick of hers—
And tried to keep her eyes upon the ground,
But vainly, for, despite what she could do,
They would glance up into the stranger's face.

She little knew who 'twas she thus did see—
That it was Loosealot, darling of the Court,
Loved of the loveliest, who had broken hearts,
E'en as his ancestors had broken heads.

The talk went on, and soon it did leak out
That at the Court Sir Smith had often been ;
That he was crony of the Coming K——.
" O, then, Sir Smith, pray tell us," cried old Brown,
" Of Guelpho's glorious deeds."   And Loosealot
    spoke,
And answered him at full, as having been
With Guelpho in his frolics many a time ;
And so he told them of his princely freaks ;
Of how he loved to bring unto his home
The lion " comiques " of the Music Halls ;
How there, before a privileged lot of chums,
They would go through their roystering *repertoire*,
And sing of " Perfect Cures," " Niersteiner Neds,"
Of " Reckless Rams," and " Nancies in the Strand."

He told of Merry Mash, of Prance the Cad,

And of the mighty George, the snob of snobs.

He also told how much the Coming K——

Enjoyed an evening at a London fire ;

How well he liked to flirt, how well to dress,

How well to dine, how well to pigeons shoot.

"Ah, yes," he said, "it is indeed a sight

To see him at the post at Hurlingham

Shoot at the head of all his Carpet Knights ;

To see the pigeons—he would miss at first,

But now's improved—come fluttering through the
        air ;

To see them fall, enough for many pies ;

To hear him shout with pleasure when they fall,

For, placid though he seems at home, and though

Not a great hand at study or at work,

Yet in his recreation few can match

Him for his zeal : *I* never saw the like."

And so they talked ; and fair Delaine, the flirt,

Lifted her eyes and read his lineaments,

And found more interest in them by far
Than in a Mudie's average "three vol."
She liked his face, though it was marked and marr'd
With blows from cricket-ball and polo sticks;
Though it was bronzed with Brighton's burning sun.
The arch-coquette was overcome at last,
And loved him, with that love which was her doom.

That night Delaine dreamt much of Loosealot,
For, going to supper, he had squeezed her hand,
And whispered pretty things going up the stairs—
He being an arrant flirt, and meaning naught,
She being for once paid out in her own coin.
So all night long his face before her lived,
Dark, splendid, speaking in the silence, full
Of noble things, and held her from her sleep.
And much she tossed upon her palliasse,
And rose next morn with rings around her eyes.
But Loosealot slept, nor dreamed of her at all;
But in the visions which appeared to him

Fleet Goanveer was present, and he saw
Her, in imagination, pass the post
A head and neck before the second horse.

Morn broke, and breakfast came ; and at the meal
All met and talked about the morning's news,
And cracked the egg, and bit anchovy toast,
And dallied with the bacon and the rolls.
Delaine had put a muslin wrapper on,
Bound with red ribbon, white and manifold,
And served the coffee with a trembling hand,
Filling poor Loosealot's cup with sugar-lumps,
And giving Nicholas no single knob.
Talk turned again upon the Tournament.
" Papa," said Sam, " I'd like to go and see
What 'tis they do ; I really should, indeed."
" So ye will grace me," put in Loosealot
(Although in heart much bored by Samuel Brown),
" Then were I glad of you as guide and friend ;
For I know nothing of transpontine town.

More, you shall shoot, and win the cup perchance,

And bring it to your sister, if you like."

Then she upset the milk-jug in her haste,

And flush'd and simper'd when she heard her name.

At last, Old Brown, all punctual, arose,

Took hat and stick and journeyed citywards,

Whither had Nicholas preceded him,

Self-conscious, on the box-seat of a 'bus.

Anon said Loosealot, " 'Tis time we went."

And Delaine, hearing that, was sad at heart.

" Could you," he did continue, " dear Miss Brown,

Lend me a small umbrella? Mine is large

And cumbersome, and yet methinks 'twill rain ;

Your brother shall return it." Ere he'd done

She'd flown upstairs and back had come again,

Bearing her own umbrella, lithe and light.

" Take it, Sir Smith," she said, " and when it rains

Then open it, and think of poor Delaine ;

Yours shall be hostage for it." And she took

His " gamp" umbrageous, and bestowed him hers.

Nor was this all ; for she had deftly picked

A dainty rosebud nestling in its moss

(For standard roses grew behind Brown's house),

And now upon her flashed the wild desire

That he should wear it in his buttonhole.

" Sir Smith," she said, all nervous, " will you wear

This rosebud in your coat?" Then, "Nay," said he,

" My dear Miss Brown, I never do wear flowers."

In truth, they cost more than he could afford.

" Yea, so," she said (a woman's whim she had

To talk like this), " why, then, in wearing mine

You will confer more honour upon me."

" Well, well," he said, not caring to be rude ;

" Well, I will wear it ; pin it in for me."

And this she did, in his left button-hole.

And all her face went scarlet like to blood,

And twice she pricked her fingers very much.

Then brother Sam said, laughing, " Sister, dear,

For fear your brother never should return—

H

Once, twice, and thrice; now get you to your work."
So kissed her and went out.   But Loosealot stayed
A moment's space, and kissed her too, then went.
And thus they mov'd away.   She stay'd a minute,
Then quietly made for the front gate, and there—
Her dyed hair blown about her powder'd face,
With quite a mark where Loosealot's lips had been—
Paused, leaning on the umbrella he had left,
In silence, while she watched them hail a cab,
Get in, and dip below the Clapham Rise.
Then to her bedroom with the "gamp" she clomb,
There kept it, and so lived in fantasy.

Meanwhile the new companions rode away
Far down the interminable Clapham Road,
Until they reached the Park of Kennington;
Whence, going straight on, gained the "Elephant,"
And tarried there a little space for beer.
But when the Bridge of Waterloo was passed
And they were blocked up in the busy Strand,

The umbrella rose before the cabman's sight,

Who stopped, and, being paid, his fares stepp'd out.

They lunched, then made on foot for Portland Road,

And, when the next train broke from underground,

And shot red fire and shadows in its wake,

They booked for Shepherd's Bush, and took their
    seats,

And with a slamming volley went their way

Until they reached the point of their desires.

Then Loosealot became the guide, and led

His *protégé*, by short and cunning cuts,

To where an avenue ope'd on the road ;

Here was a gate, and here a keeper stood

Who took half-sovereigns of both ; for he

Knew not Sir Loosealot in his disguise.

Inside, they found themselves 'midst well-dressed
    folks,

'Midst carriages and horses, cabs and brough'ms ;

'Midst spanking " tits," and stylish four-in-hands ;

So on, till next a mansion barred the way,

Passing through which they to a garden came,

By oaken fencing bounded.   Passing this,

They gained the meadow where the match was shot.

To Sam the sight was new ; so he gazed hard

Upon the scene of pomp and chivalry.

He saw the ropes which ran around the lists ;

The ladies dotted o'er the soft green sward,

Like some bright rainbow fall'n on the grass.

He saw the traps—a row stood on the ground—

In these the foes the Knights were soon to meet.

And there were wicker baskets full of birds,

Who all would have to struggle for their lives.

" You well may look," to Sam said Loosealot ;

" It is indeed a chivalrous affray ;

We Knights "—and here he pointed to the groups

Of stalwart men who stalked about the turf—

" Have, gun in hand, to fight those fierce wild
     birds. '

And Sam he looked again, and Sam he saw

It was a rare and noble company ;

For half *Debrett* was there.   You could have made

A quorum of the Lower House ; and Peers

Were thick as pink-tipped daisies in the grass ;

Lords jostled Dukes ; and Dukes on Barons trod ;

And German Princes mustered in great force.

Moreover, 'neath a tent pitched in the shade,

Sam, warned by Loosealot, saw the coming K——,

In suit complete of Shetland homespun robed.

His open face, his laughing, bright blue eye

Told of no trouble, no official care ;

But loud he laughed him with his fav'rite Knight,

What time he sucked a cobbler through a straw,

Nor thought he of the coming conflict dread.

" There," said great Loosealot to his young friend,

" There is our chief, there is the Coming K——,

The worthy leader of our every game.

He sets our fashions.   He a brother has

Who has invented for us a new drink.

He has a lion heart ; he has no fear

When Knight meets dove, and comes the pull of

    string ;

The pull's for us, you see, and not for them.

He knocks the billiard balls about unmoved,

And watches polo with a calm, brave face ;

His courage such, it carries him well through

The thickest mazes of a crowded ball ;

He sits out plays with unmatched hardihood ;

He dines with valour full of fearlessness ;

He lays large sums, and numberless first stones,

(Though he throws none) with mason's skill and

    trowel.

He is indeed a pattern knight to us.

There is the man." And young Brown gazed upon

    him

As on a thing miraculous. But, anon,

A gun was fired, and then did either side—

They that assail'd and they that were attack'd—

Prepare the war. The pigeons in their traps ;

The Knights about a post, with guns in hand.

A serving-man, in velveteen arrayed,

With many strings his fingers twisted round,

Pulls one. A trap is opened, and flies out

A pigeon, yearning, straining to be free.

Skyward it mounts, as though to plead its cause

At heaven's gate. Such orisons are naught.

A Knight is at the firing peg; the stock

Is at his shoulder. Suddenly he fires:

There is a flash, a crack; the hard earth shakes,

And falls the dove down dead—a mangled mass.

So is the Tournament commenced, and so

It does go on, with variation small.

Sometimes the bird is missed, sometimes so hit

That it just gets away to linger on

A few sharp hours of pain amongst the ferns.

And all the while the swell of music sounds,

And dresses *frou-frou*, and the ladies talk,

And ices pass around, and beauty smiles

Upon the *pigeontry* of Guelpho's Knights.

Long time young Brown looked on, then turned and
    said

To Loosealot, "Oh, what glorious sport is this!

What gallantry, what valiant daring 'tis!

Now know I how dove-voted you knights are."

And Loosealot smiled complacent at the pun;

Then, after some more shooting, went him up

And claimed his turn.   Said all, "Who can this
    be?"

But, hearing that his name was Smith, they ceased

To wonder further, and he had his turn,

And many a turn.   And so it came to pass

That every bird he shot at, that he slew.

Knight looked at knight, and even Guelpho stared

To see the stranger—for they twigged him not—

Out-do the doughtiest knight upon the ground.

"He shoots like Loosealot," said one; "but he

Is Smith!   I've surely heard that name before."

And yet he was not known.   And when it came

To be the final and deciding tie,

He took sure aim, and trigger pulled, and then
Fell heavily; for, lo! the barrel burst.

Then did young Brown right well and worshipfully—
Warm was the heart beneath his city clothes—
And brought assistance to where Loosealot lay,
And bore him tenderly unto a cab.
And, as he lay all sweating with his pain,
One came to say that he had won the prize,
And brought a silver vase, répoussé work,
Saying, " Behold the cup which Guelpho sends."
"The cup!" poor Loosealot answer'd; " don't cup
      me,
But give, for God's love, me a little air."
And so it came to pass that in the haste
The cabman got the cup and stuck to it ;
But Loosealot, o'ercome with pain, cared not,
And so they drove him to the Albany.

When he was gone, and it was buzzed about—

" Heaven hinder," said the Coming K——, " that
    he,

As great a knight as we have seen to-day,

Should pass uncared for.   Wherefore rise, I say,

O Equerry, and go and find the knight.

I charge you say I'm sorry for his wound,

And tell him my physician shall be his ;

And bring us where he is, and how he fares ;

But if you fail, then advertise at once,

And put the 'cute Pollaky on the track."

So forth the equerry went, but was too late

To trace the hansom which bore Loosealot ;

So next day advertised, somewhat this way :—

" If this should meet the eye of him who won

The Challenge Cup at Hurlingham, and was,

By bursting rifle, sorely wounded, then

Let him apply or send to the Gun Club,

And it to his advantage will conduce."

The charge for which was seven-and-six at least.

No morning passed, or it was wet or dry,
But at the Clapham Rise abode of Brown
A ragged urchin called, and, with a shout,
Flung down the *Telegraph* into the hall.
The second morning from the one when Sam
And Loosealot left Sam's sister at the gate
Had dawned, and Sam had not come back as yet ;
And Brown the father was full much incensed,
Bidding in mental language to go hang
The handsome stranger who led off his boy.
Bnt fair Delaine dwelt still in fantasy,
And sat for hours to guard his cherished " gamp,"
And made a case for it of shabby silk,
Neglecting her house duties and her pa,
And kept the one-day-seen one in her heart.

The second morning came, as has been writ ;
It brought its *Telegraph* as sure as day.
Now so it chanced Delaine was in the hall,
And took it up, all listless, with a glance

To see if yet the Queen had come to Court,

And, turning it, the notice caught her eye

Detailed already somewhere farther back.

" Can it be he ? " she thought, " the man I love ? "

Then took the *Telegraph* to her papa,

And poured his coffee in the butter-dish,

And put, unconsciously, milk on his fish ;

Then, when his melancholy meal was made,

Crept to his side before he rose to go,

Sat on his knee, pulled his grey beard, and said,

" Papa, you call me flighty, and the word

Is not, perhaps, this morning misapplied ;

But can you wonder that I lose my wits ? "

" I have some wonder at the thought," he said ;

" 'Tis whether you have any wits to lose."

At which she resolutely pulled his beard,

And said, " O, pa, it's all about poor Sam.

Where can he be ? what doing can he be ? "

Which saying, the false maiden sighed, and rubbed

The corners of her mischief-making eyes.

" Oh, oh ! " said Mr. Brown, " then this is it ?

Good girl, to think about your brother thus.

He is all right, no doubt." " But, pa," she said,

" Let me this morning go in search of him.

I want to shop a bit in Regent Street,

And then I'll see if he is at Aunt Smith's,

In Saville Row." Then, nodding his assent,

Her father went toward the teeming town.

But she, her suit allow'd, slipt soft away,

And dressed her in a Dolly Varden suit,

Kissed the umbrella, and, by tram and 'bus,

Made for the occidental end of town.

As fate would have it—here it should be said

How favourable to poets fate e'er is—

Scarce had she turned from Regent Street to go

To her Aunt Smith's, when she her brother met ;

Whom when she saw, " O, Sam ! " she cried, " O,
        Sam !

How fares Sir Smith to-day ? " And he, amazed,

" Sister Delaine! why here ?   How is Sir Smith !
Why he, my dear, is better, on the whole.
I have just left the doctor at his door,
And for two days I have been nursing him."
" Oh," said his sister, " what would I not give
To look upon his handsome face again ! "
But thus her brother, " 'Twould not proper be
For you within the Albany to go.
Go home, good girl, and I will tell Sir Smith
You have with much concern inquired for him ;
And tell the guv'nor that I'm all serene."
So did they part ; but still Delaine remained,
And hovered near, and saw her brother go
Adown the glass-roofed corridor, and then
Turn sharply through a door and disappear.

Then went she home by 'bus and tram again,
Far through the road of Clapham to her kin.
But oft, day after day, she used to pass—
Pretending 'twas her old Aunt Smith to see—

Across the river to the western parts,
In happy hope that she Sir Smith might see ;
But did not for a while ; for long he lay
Brain-feverous in his pain and agony.
And the great knight in his mid-sickness made
Full many a vow at doves no more to shoot,
But henceforth would be true to Goanveer,
And her alone ; and so in time got well.
Soon after, fate so brought it, on a day
When Delaine was, as usual, at the West,
He, walking slowly, met her in the street,
And paused, and thanked her for her kind concern ;
And, for blood ran lustier in him now,
Called her the sweet Delaine, and made her blush.
Before they parted he with her arranged
Another meeting, for he liked the girl,
And thought, " Till I am well enough to go
And look entirely after Goanveer,
She will amuse me." So they often met—
Brown knowing naught—and oft he wrote to her.

But when at last his hurt was wholly well,
And Epsom meeting loomed quite close at hand,
He told her on a day, " To-morrow morn
I go, and I shall never see you more."
Then suddenly and passionately she spoke :
" I have gone mad. I love you. 'Tis leap-year."
" Ah, sister," answer'd Loosealot, " what is this ? "
A safe thing on the whole for him to say.
And she, " You know full well, you cruel man."
Then he again, " What fantasy is this ?
You've walked with me, and I have walked with you ;
We both have walked about each with the other ;
But surely that is naught ; for you must know
I'm not at all a marrying sort of man."
Whereat her eyes flashed fire, and she'd have said
Some bitter words ; but he had passed away.

So in her room alone the maiden sat :
Her lord was gone, but his umbrella stayed,
And for a time she felt his absence much,

But soon plucked up a spirit and looked through
His heap of letters, haply there to find
Some promise definite to marry her,
That she might bring a breach of promise on.
But yet, she being a Clapham girl—not one
Of those fair creatures who but live in song—
She did not leave her meals, or get no sleep,
Or hear strange voices in the moaning wind ;
She did not fast and take her dresses in,
Or weep and take religious volumes out
From Mudie's.　No, she calmly bode her time,
And cherished in her heart a sure revenge.

Now in those days she made a little song,
And call'd her song, "The Song of One who Flirts,"
And sang it.　Sweetly could she make and sing :

" True love is nonsense ; there is no such thing ;
　Flirting is jolly, 'tis of that I sing ;
　　I won't go in for true love, no, not I.

" Love, are you sweet ?   No, no, from meals you
        keep.

  Love, are you bitter?   Yes, you spoil one's sleep.

    O Love ! this maiden means not you to try.

" But flirting never makes one fade away ;

  Can't flirt too long, it's sure some day to pay ;

    I mean to flirt henceforward, that do I.

" I might have loved, but that was not to be ;

  I'll flirt with all the men that I can see ;

    Come, some one, let me flirt, or I shall die."

Meantime was Loosealot with Goanveer,

And never thought of Sam or of Delaine ;

But it had been discovered at the Court

That he and brave Sir Smith were both the same ;

And he explained to Guelpho his disguise,

And why he'd practised on his prince deceit,

Who, chiding him, forgave him o'er his wine,

And drank his health in various foreign brands.
Moreover, some impulsive underling,
Hearing the story, put it in the *Post*,
Whence it was copied by the common prints,
And Delaine read it ; and she was fresh vexed
A prize so valuable had her escaped,
And read her letters carefully again,
To see if they did not contain some word
That could by Vallantyne be turned to use.

But, failing in her search—for he'd been 'cute—
She did not fall to moaning or to mope ;
Nor did she paler grow, or want to die,
But still resolved on " having " him somehow.

It came to pass, at last, that on a day
The Coming K—— announced a garden fête,
And bid a host of fashionable guests :
And Loosealot and all the Knights were bid,
And all the high-born ladies of the Court ;

Which came unto the ears of fair Delaine,
Who, to herself, said, " Now my time is come."

So, when the day came round, she sat and penned,
With face all bright with smiles, a lengthy note,
Which, being writ, she folded it, and put
It in her pocket ; then she donned her best,
Her prettiest blue silk, with polonaise
Of some aërial fabric, and a sash
Of ribbon blue as laughing lassie's eye,
Or pa's shaved chin upon a frosty morn.
Next, taking Loosealot's letters and his flowers,
She packed them up, and then the umbrella took—
His green umbrella, battered and obese—
And, slipping out, got in a four-wheel cab
And bade the Jehu drive her to the Mall.
He was a gnarled old driver on the box,
With blinking eyes, and twisted all his face,
And dirty hands, and features far from clean,
But yet polite withal ; so jumped he down,

And helped her in, and on her closed the door ;
Then mounted he again, and so the fare,
Driv'n by the foul, went upward to the Mall.

The fête was at its height, the smooth-shaved turf
Was covered with high dames, with lusty lords ;
With all of Guelpho's Dinner Table Knights.
The merry jest went round ; the strawberry
Mashed in Devonshire " clotted " did the same :
The iced-cream sodas frothed in flavoured glee ;
Cliquot and Moët bubbled in the sun,
And Guelpho was in most transcendent " form,"
To all most affable, as was his wont.
For all the guests the Coming K—— prepared
A cold collation, but a welcome warm.
And Northerland was there, and Coachington,
And meek Sir Dormount and the bold Heraint,
With Shenid near him, as you may be sure.
Near to his Prince was Loosealot the keen,
The hero of our tournament and tale ;

And much they talked in whispers of their mare,

Of Goanveer the matchless and the fleet.

For then the Coming K—— knew ne'er a word

Of the great wrong that Loosealot had planned,

And the deceit that he had compasséd.

So sped the fête; but little thought the guests

The Clapham cab was speeding too the while,

And making for St. James's.

                            But the cab

On to the Guelphic Garden crawling, paused.

There two stood arm'd, and kept the gate; and they

Looked at the cabman's gnarled and dirty face,

And said, "What is it?" adding, "Who goes
        there?"

But he no word did answer, for his fare,

Alighting, swept the pavement with her skirts,

And—having made him glad with florins twain—

Walked boldly to the gate, to those on guard.

"I'm fair Delaine," she said, "of Clapham Rise;

I come to look for Loosealot at the fête."
So saying, went she through, while their mouths
    gaped,
And thus she passed into the garden grounds.

All up the yellow gravel paths she passed,
In her right hand the umbrella, in her left
The letter—all her brown hair streaming down ;
And all her polonaise was crêpe de Chine,
Drawn to the waist, and full and puffed behind,
Chaussure and skirt of blue ; and for her face,
That was pure white, for she had powdered it.
With footstep measured and a face demure,
She minced her way, till came a sound of chat
And babble on the breeze ; then halted she.
Now, girt with knights, round corner proximate
Came Guelpho, and his courtiers following.
Sir Loosealot was there, and saw she him ;
Saw he her too—all present did the same ;
And not an eye but asked, "Who is it, then ?"

For there she stood mysterious, and held·
The bulky green umbrella out at length,
Pointing it straight at great-gun Loosealot.
" Who is it ? " cried they all ; and Guelpho turned
To Loosealot ; but Loosealot turned pale ;
And then Delaine, thus challenged, took three
    strides,
Stood all defiant 'fore the Coming K——.
In sinister hand the letter then she took,
Stooped, broke the seal, and read it : thus she read,
And all the time at Loosealot did point :
" Most noble Knight, Sir Smith, or Loosealot—
Since you are pleased to have an alias—
I, sometime called Delaine, of Clapham Rise,
Come, for you left me taking no farewell,
Hither to take my last farewell of you.
I loved you, and you only played me false ;
But do not think my love will be my death.
I hate you now, but I may not forget
I still have your umbrella ; here it is ! "

At this she opened it—a sorry sight.

"This, then, I bring you, for perhaps 'twill do
To guard the head of cherished Goanveer.
Here, too"—and then she took the packet out—
"Are all your letters and your trump'ry flowers.
Take it and them!"   With which, like Amazon
Who flings with doomful aim the poisoned dart,
Or as a schoolboy, fresh from tedious tasks,
Propels the unboiled adamantine pea,
She launched the green umbrella at him full,
And met him with the ferule in the chest;
Then followed with the packet, which, well sent,
Landed on "chimney pot," and knocked it off.
And ever as this happened lords and dames
Laughed, looking often from her face who read
To his she read at, which was pale with rage;
And ever Guelpho tittered at his plight;
And not a knight but teased and rallied him;
But worse the ladies, who all looked upon
The fair Delaine as champion of their sex.

So, when he had recovered from his blows,

The Coming K—— began to speak, and said,

" O Loosealot, my Loosealot (pray pull

Yourself together, Loosealot), in whom

I mostly put my faith " (and here he wank),

" Who hast in many adventures been with me,

Passed many an hour at gay Cremorne *incog.*,

And merriiy gone roving through the town;

I knew thou wert a dog, but never guessed

Thou wert so bad a dog as now turns out.

O, Loosealot " (here he poked him in the ribs),

" How could'st thou serve the Clapham maiden so ?

Thy punishment is meet.   And now see to't,

The girl some luncheon has now that she is here;

I bid thee see that she lunch worshipfully."

So towards a buffet rich in cakes and wine

Loosealot unwilling led Delaine the fair,

All sheepishly, and could not find his tongue;

But she, not bearing malice towards him now,

Did rally him to crackers pull with her,

And chaffed, " I hope I did not hurt you much."
And presently, all merry with champagne,
Went back and mingled with the noble throng,
Flirted with many knights, incensed their dames,
And ere she left had kissed the Coming K——.

'Tis writ in chronicles the writer's seen
That fair Delaine was wed within the year
To one named Quarterlow, a city knight,
Who stands a chance some day to be Lord Mayor ;
But he who writes this page, says, Cousin Smith.
Yet, any way, she never feels regret
For Loosealot, who is not what he was
Since Goanveer—— But we anticipate.
Enough to know, it never is forgot
How he was shown up at the garden fête ;
And 'tis ne'er likely he will hear the last
Of fair Delaine and the umbrella green.

THE GLASS OF ALE.

THE GLASS OF ALE.

FROM fisticuffs and acts of prowess done
In many a prize-ring, Johnny Walkingshaw,
Whom Guelpho loved to call The Nobbly One,
Had passed unto a quiet village pub,
The " Fox and Goose," and leaving for the bar
The noble art of self-defence, had come
To Ducklington, there settled for his life.
And one, a villager among the rest,
Tom Dobbin, loved him much beyond the rest,
And worshipt him ; and never missed a day
But what he came to drink him of his beer ;
And looked on him with awe, for he had heard,
Of all the prowess of the Nobbly One,
And loved to hear him tell of his great deeds,
And listened reverently and stood him drink.

One Sabbath afternoon in June, they sat

Outside the public, underneath the sign,
And quaff'd the pewter and filled up the pipe ;
Then puffed the curling smoke into the clouds
Above them ; and as there they sat
Tom Dobbin questioned Walkingshaw, and said :
" O, Johnny, I have seen you sit and smoke,
Day after day, for close upon six months,
And I have heard, indeed full well I know,
You once had favour with the Coming K—— ;
But never have I known or have you told
What 'twas that made you come and settle here.
O, Johnny ! was it love of solitude ? "
" Nay," said the Nobbly One, " it were not that,
I don't go in for no such foolish lay.
The truth is, guv'nor " (here he slapped his side),
" I found my wind weren't what it used to be,
So I knocked under, scratched myself, yer know,
And left the purfesshnul for the public line.
'Tis true I wasn't beat ; no, never since
I beat the Poplar Pet in sixty-six ;

But, as I said, my wind was touched, and so,
As I had got the champion-belt, thinks I
I'll keep it; so I just bought this here pub,
And came down here to hend my days in peace."

To whom Tom said: "The champion-belt! you
     say;
I never knew before that it was yours;
Though oft have I heard of it; and full oft
Have longed to see it.   Could you show it me?"

"In course I can," said Johnny Walkingshaw.
Then rose and disappeared within the Inn;
Went creaking up the passage to the door
That opened on the room behind the bar—
A little room with old oak wainscoting,
And settles by the wide-mouthed fireplace set;
And all the walls were covered with designs
Of sporting subjects, brightly-coloured prints
Of famous "cracks" who'd pulled great races off;

And portraits of the " fancy " : huge-jowled men,

With beefy necks, short hair and high cheek-
    bones,

And noses of the most eccentric shapes.

Upon the side-board was a terrier stuffed,

Who for a wager had killed many rats,

Flanked either side by ample loving-cups

And goblets, trophies of great triumphs won;

But o'er the mantle-board was placed a case

Made of mahogany, with front of glass;

And inside this was kept the champion's belt—

A velvet zone, with silver much beset,

Which showed in bas-relief what John had done,

And spoke in graven letters of his fame.

This reaching down, he (Walkingshaw is meant)

Placed it beneath his arm—his stalwart arm

On which the standing muscle still did slope,

As slopes a wild brook o'er a little stone,

Running too vehemently to break upon it—

And so went out and showed it unto Tom.

" So this," said Dobbin, " is the champion's belt—
The champion-belt itself, for which you've fought,
For which you've bled and gone about with
     bumps
Upon your features, and your eyes in black ? "

To whom the Nobbly One : " Exactly so.
This is the belt, you may depend on that.
I winned it fair enough off Mauling Matt,
As beat the ' Chicken ' but a week afore.
And work enough it were to win it, too,
With one eye bunged up and one mauley strained.
But, there, I did it fair, and that's enough."

" Nay, worthy Walkingshaw," did he reply,
Who, rustic-hearted, longed to hear of " life,"
" Tell me, I pray you, more of this same fight,
And more of how you managed Mauling Matt.
Meanwhile, ho ! tapster ! bring a pewter forth
Charged to the brim with your most potent ale ;

For well I know, O noted Nobbly One,

You cannot tell me if your throat be dry."

So came the ale, and with a sounding gulp

The " Nobbly " wet his throat ; and so he said :

" Let's see, it must be full five year ago ;

The fight was fust arranged one night at Nat's ;

I'd dropped in all promiscus like, to see

If anything was on, and have a drain,

When up comes Nat and whispers in my ear,

' The swells is here in force to-night, old pal,

And wants to get a mill up ; are yer game ? '

' Try me,' says I, and gived my reg'lar wink,

As means whole wollums when yer knows it well.

' All right,' says he, ' come in along with me ;

I'll introduce yer to the Coming K——.'

I took a nip to calm my ruffled 'eart,

Then followed Nat to see the Coming K——.

The parlour were chuck full o' heavy swells ;

O' Lords, and Wiscounts, and o' Barrownites ;

And up one end was Guelpho, him I knowed
Immediate by his phiz; so Nat spoke up;
Said he, ' Your Ryle 'Ighness, 'ere's a man
As'll fight Old Nick hisself, if that was all.'
At that they all cried ' Brayvo,' and one swell
Said, ' He's the man for Mauling Matt, I think ' ;
And Guelpho nodded, and they cheered agin,
And giv me champagne in a silver cup."

Then spoke Tom Dobbin, curious, asking him,
" What said the Coming K——? Did he not
    speak ? "

" O, yes," said Walkingshaw, " the Coming K——
Were most polite and haffable, I'm sure ;
He shook my ' mauley ' like a honest man,
And said 'ow glad he were to meet with me.
' Which I'm the same to meet your grace,' I says,
' An' 'opes as all at 'ome is werry well.'
At which he winked, and all the swell 'uns grinned ;

And so the merry toast and joke went round.
Say what you like, that Guelpho's a good sort,
And all 'is fav'rite knights are proper 'uns.

Well, 'fore we left that night, 'twas all arranged,
As 'ow the ' mill ' should be, and when, and where,
And half the stakes was put down there and then,
And given to a gent from Mother Bell's."

Then he who listed : " Did the mill come off ? "
And he who told : " Now, don't you hinterrupt !

I went in training when the sun next broke
From underground ; 'twas on a Saturday ;
And all went well until the morning come
When I should go to pot or win the belt.
We'd kept the secret wonderfully well,
And not a blessed ' bobby ' knew on it ;
Or, if one did, he'd been a-squared all right.
And Lunnon Bridge was made our ' rundy-voo.'

Thanks to the Coming K——, a special train
Were waiting for us, and I went first class,
With Guelpho, and Sir Loosealot, Heraint,
And horsey Coachington, and gay Sir Gower.
I were in prime condition ; not a hounce
Of surplice flesh, and muscles 'ard as stones,
As Guelpho felt 'em as we journey'd down.
My second was the ' Walworth Slogger ' ; he
Had got the sponge and brandy in a bag ;
And Matt was in another carriage with
His backers, and the blinds drawed careful down.
'Twas just past Erith that the train drawed up ;
A death-white mist were rising on the Thames,
Whereof the chill to him who breathed it caused
A tickling of his diaphragm, and so
We all set coughing like asthmatic sheep.
And fell the mist o'er all the fields, until
Our way was lost, and some fell in the ditch.
But brake the sun at last, and then we pitched
The ropes, and fixt the stakes into the ground ;

And then the people circled all the lists,

Some squatting on their haunches, some upright.

The seat of honour were the Coming K———'s,

And beamingly he gazed upon the scene,

And whispered in my ear afore the fight,

' The belt will be for thee,'; 'twas this he said ;

And I, too, echoed, ' Yes ; 'twill be for me ! '

So then the seconds for our corners tossed,

And Matt got 'is right facing to the sun ;

And then we stripped, shook mauleys, and forthwith

The combat for the championship beginned.

What happened, 'taint for me to say, in course ;

But here's *Bell's Life* with all the rounds writ down

(So saying, drew he from his pocket out

A sheet of newspaper) ; read it yourself ! "

And passing it to Dobbin, Dobbin read :

" There, then, they stood, two brawny Englishmen,

Hight ' Mauling Matt,' and John the ' Nobbly One.'

Some paces parted them, and, 'tween their feet,

The pink-tipped daisy lifted up its head ;
But this they heeded not, but, with set mouths,
Each clenched his bunch of fives, and danced about
The other delicately, with a tread
Like tread of cats who walk upon hot bricks.
First with the left did one let out, and then
The other ; still they only beat the air ;
Till, presently, the Nobbly One ran in,
Swift as a wild wave in the wild North Sea,
And placed, with more than gentle force, his right
Between the other's eyes, and kept it there,
Till Matt drew back, not relishing the jest,
And, over eager, fell upon his back.
With that came forth a long and lusty cheer ;
And there were loud cries for the ' Nobbly One.'
The Coming K——— himself did clap his hands,
And booked a bet of four to one on John.
What time Matt's second took him on his knee,
And sponged his face, and gave him alcohol.
Again the twain confronted, each to each ;

Again the cat-on-hot-brick movement tried ;
And lo ! Matt's forehead bore a budding bump,
And glow'd his face like a great fire at Yule,
So riled was he with passion, crying out,
' Come on, O Nobbly One.'   And so he came,
And thrice they closed, and thrice did separate ;
Then each, with windmill arms, hit out at each
So often and with such blows, that all the crowd
Wonder'd, and now and then, all round the rope,
There was a clapping as of many hands.
But still they fought, not heeding blows, and
     still
The dew of their great labour, and the blood
Of their squat noses, flowing, drain'd their force.
But either's force was match'd till Guelpho's cry,
' Remember, Nobbly One, for what you fight ! '
Increased his man's, who got his left well on,
Smashed Matt's teeth in his mouth, and with the
     blow
Fell'd him.   And this concluded round the second.

Then, spluttering through his hedge of splinter'd
  teeth,
Came ' Mauling Matt ' still gamely up to ' Time ' ;
But he was seeming ' groggy ' on his pins,
And sawed the air with vigour purposeless.
The waiting game the Nobbly One then tried,
And let him waste his strength, nor said him nay,
And, waiting for a chance, rushed in at times,
More claret spilled, or dotted, p'raps, an eye,
Whilst there were bets on him of ten to one.
So went the fight for thirty minutes' space ;
And not a round, but Matt did fare the worse.
Still, pluckily did he come up to time,
And managed, now and then, by happy fluke,
To mar the details of John's frontispiece.
But his own mother, had she met poor Matt,
Would not have known him for her eldest boy ;
So changed was he beneath the Nobbly's fists.

  * * * * *

Round seventeen began. With eyes bunged up,

And nose all flattened on his gory face,

Matt faced his foe once more ; or, as 'tis writ

In sporting parlance, ' Smiling he came up '

(Though he who tells the tale would like to know

If beefsteak can be said to smile at all).

The Nobbly One, save for a cut or two,

And one black eye, and one loose tooth or so,

Was all upon the spot, and stood to win.

Then fight was joined, and ' Nobbly ' was the cry

That filled the damp and marshy atmosphere.

It nerved him, seemingly, for in a trice,

While yet the round was young, he made

But one full bound, and brought his left well home

On Matt's raw temples, and forthwith Matt fell,

Like to a log, and lay upon the turf.

Then did gay Guelpho clap his hands with glee,

And pat the Nobbly One upon his back ;

' O noble man,' he said, ' and chivalrous :

Almost I feel inclined to dub thee knight,

For grandly hast thou fought thy fight to-day,
And well have I pulled off my bets on thee.
Who says the days of knightly deeds are done ?'
(And here he pointed at Matt's senseless form.)
' All hail the modern tournament ! say I.'
So they ' all hailed ' it ; and went back to town ;
And, later, Walkingshaw received the belt,
And keeps it, from attack inviolate.
But ' Mauling Matt,' his hurts being serious,
Took to his bed, and in a fortnight passed."

"So ho !" said Dobbin, as he reached the end,
"This, then, is how you gained the champion-belt.
Sir, I admire you," and he shook his hand,
And called for more old ale, and drank his health.
Then questioned him still further, and he said,
"So you had knowledge of the Coming K——;
Say, was he, as 'tis rumoured, pretty right ?"

To whom the Nobbly One : "I know'd him well,

And call him an uncommon jolly sort.

No pride, nor stuck-up nonsense, have he got ;

He is a man I'm proud to call my ' pal.'

As for being ' fast,' why 'taint for me to say

What pace he went at.   This, though, coves told me,

It all depended on his chums ; if they

Went racing on, why he went racing too,

But if they drov'd it mild, *he* drov'd it mild.

He's like a potter's wessel, which turns out

Whatever shape the potter wants it to.

His Knights go it above a bit, yer see,

And they makes him the same ; that's all the truth.

If his Papa had lived, quite likely then

He might ha' got into a different set,

Gone in for preaching in the open air,

Or p'rhaps ha' been a ritualistic cove,

Or took delight in buildin' 'alls and shows,

Or givin' lectures to good workin' men ;

But as his Pa was nipped in the bud,

It turned out otherwise.   But what I says

Is, wild oats must be sowed ; so 'taint no good
To bother 'cos he's sowed a tidyish crop."

" Just so," the villager replied, " you have
Full reason, landlord, in the words you speak."

But here the landlord rose with anxious mien,
And much concern was figured in his face.
" Go to, O guest," he cried, " it's three o'clock,
And by the law my public must be closed."

With sigh long drawn, the villager arose ;
But as he stood there came a sound of hoofs,
And, rounding from behind a barley-mow,
A troop of mounted gallants rode in sight.
One, two, three, four, five, six, they rode in view,
And reined in, clattering, by the public's door.

" Ho, landlord ! " cried out one, " see to our steeds,
And we would drink us of thy oldest ale ! "

" We would," the other five in chorus cried.

And all aghast the landlord raised his hands.

" Now woe is me, O gentlemen ! " he cried ;

" I dare not serve you, for my house is closed,

Save you are *bony-fidy* travellers,

And can your railway-tickets all produce."

" What nonsense ! " spoke the one who spoke before.

" Travellers !   Of course, we are, else why we here ?

But tickets !   On my soul, you are a wag.

Tickets !   We ride, and do not come by train."

To whom the Nobbly One : " Alas ! alas !

And woe is all of us, and lack-a-day !

The police has giv' the office as to what

A *bony-fidy* is.   I must take heed

To their instruction.   You can't have no ale ! "

Then got each gallant down from off his horse :

Tied was each horse unto a neighbouring fence :

And, sitting round the table, all began

To bluster for refreshment.   But he spake
(The one who spake before) and said, "Shut up!
And let me tell the landlord here a tale.

But yesterday I stood in Guelpho's Halls,
And talked with him on publics and their signs,
Talked we, 'midst other matters, of the Act
Which lately, host, you know, has come to pass.
And Guelpho said : ' It seems, Sir Knight, to me,
It will be hard to get a glass of ale
Henceforth.'   At which I, with my cheek aflame,
Said, 'What! are Britons to be slaves ? '   And he :
' It seems so.'   And I felt a glow uprise
Of indignation, and I shouted, ' I
Will go and get one even now, my liege ! '
' But,' said the Coming K——, ' Sir Knight, pray
        pause,
And think, before you enter on this quest.
My word for't, you will follow wandering fires ;
Be lost, p'rhaps, in the quagmire, and return

L

No more.'   But I was lifted up in heart,
And thought in such a quest I should not fail ;
And all my blood danced in me, for I felt
That I should light upon the glass of ale.

Thereafter the dark warning of my liege,
That I should only follow wandering fires,
Came like a London fog across my mind,
And I was thirsty even unto death ;
And, sad, I cried, ' The quest is not for me—'
This though 's anticipatory, O host !

But, to resume, the eve I left the Halls
Where Guelpho sat, I rushed excitedly,
With face aflame and throbbing pulse, to where
A hostelry rose glaring in the night.
Pushing the swinging doors, I entered in,
And said, ' A glass of ale ! and quickly, please,
Lest I believe the hideous thing I've heard,
That 'tis not to be had henceforth.'   At which

A potman leerily and mockingly

Said, ' Even so, you cannot, sir, be served ;

Your face is flush'd, your speech is quick, and
  so

It's evident you've had enough before.'

But for the counter, I should then and there

Have brained that potman with a pewter pot ;

But, swallowing my wrath, instead of ale,

Went furiously out into the night.

And on I went, and when I thought my thirst

Would slay me, saw another house,

All gas, and glass, and glitter, and went in.

Scarce had I called for my one glass of ale,

When on my shoulder I a finger felt,

And, turning, saw a p'liceman—Z 16.

' Look here,' he said ; ' this will not do, you know.

I saw you turned out just now from the " Crown,"

And now you try it on again.   Be off,

Or I shall " run you in."'   Speechless, well nigh,

I let him push me out; and stood alone,
And thirsting, in a land of licences.

And on I went, till, heedless what I did,
So great my anger was at what had happed,
I stumbled on a music hall, went in,
And there, in box ensconced, forgot my care,
My thirst, my anger, everything; for there,
Oblivious of the songs—most rotten things,
As most songs of the period surely are—
I slept, nor woke until the curtain fell
And all the audience went crowding out.
And out *I* went, and greater was my thirst
For being so long unsated; and I hied
Unto a hostelry; and, lo! 'twas shut.
'What! foiled again?' I cried.   'O, cursed fate!
Why, why act thus? what Nemesis is this?'
And, knocking vehemently, a policeman passed,
And said, 'Move on, young man, for don't you know
It's twelve o'clock, and, by the Act just passed,

All houses close at midnight ? ' Then I moaned,

And murmured, ' Prescient Guelpho, thou wert
    right.'

And I walked on and overtook a man

All hurrying, and I asked, ' Where, then, so fast ? '

And he, all breathless, answered, and he said,

' I go to gain an exempted public-house.'

' O, brother, I will join you,' was my cry.

And so we twain went on, and came at last

Upon a pub still open in a street,

And manifold the crowd about its doors.

' A goodly company in sooth,' I cried,

And push'd my way up nearer to the door,

Where stood a constable, who said to me,

' Whence come you, sir ? ' and even as he spake

I cried as one whose throat was very dry,

' From the Minerva Music Hall I hail ! '

' Then,' answered he, ' I cannot let you in.

Nocturnal ale is not for such as you ;

Theatre-goers only come in here.'

With muttered language, far from choice, I went,

And, mindful of my liege's words, I sped,

Till, thirsty, I reached home and sought my couch.

This morning, rising early, parched and dry,

I longed again for draughts of bitter ale,

And sent my servant—faithful crone is she—

To fill a flagon at a neighbouring inn.

You'll guess what happ'd: the wither'd crone came
    back

Without the ale; it was the Sabbath morn,

And not a public ope'd till half-past one.

Then I, impatient, jumped upon this horse,

And rode without the city, sick at heart ;

Came soon upon a brewery, so vast,

The very air was full of malt and hop ;

I could have ridden in that brewery

And plunged into a vat to slake my thirst,

But could not, for the gate was shut and barred.

'Twas porter, porter everywhere, but not
A drop to drink, much less a glassful of it.
So murmuring still, ' O, Guelpho, thou wert right ! '
I spurred my steed, and rode on, thirsty yet.
And then, behold, a woman at a door
Sitting ; and fair the house whereby she sat
With whitewash ; and her eyes were kind,
And all her bearing gracious.   She rose
When I pulled up, as who should say ' Come in ! '
And I, with reverent bow to pommel made,
Cried, ' Lady, I'm a wandering knight, athirst.'
And she : ' A knight !   Why, I'm a Templar, lad ;
My husband D. P. G. is of his lodge.'
Not knowing what she meant, nor heeding it,
I gasp'd, ' Fair lady knight, give me to drink.'
So she, with dapper step, went in the house ;
And visions of home-brewed rose in my brain ;
I could have hugged my horse's neck with joy.
And when my eyes open'd I heard her step
Falling ; I saw her, like a silver star,

Stand in the doorway, and she bore a jug
I could have worshipp'd it, for, in my thirst,
A thing of beauty and a joy to me
It was; for then I thought my time had come.
And, coming to my stirrup, she poured out—
A glass of water ! and she said, ' It is
Fresh filtered, sir, this morning ' ; and I could
Have dropped into the dust and grovelled there.
' Mistaken woman ! ' then said I, ' avaunt !
Nor tempt me with your choleraic cup.
Have you no bitter for a brother knight ?
O tell me, lady Templar, tell me true ! '

Then she : ' What ! dare you, then, Sir Knight,
        insult
The wife of a Good Templar D. P. G. ?
How is it that you do not know ere this
That water is the Templar's only drink ?
Ale is accursèd ; I would touch it not,
Nor hand it to you, e'en to save thy life.

Come, say henceforth you, too, will give it up,
And join the ranks of our pump-water band.'
With this she slipped again within the house,
To find, I fancy, a teetotal card ;
But I, gripping my charger with my knees,
Flew on, and murmured, 'Guelpho! thou wert
   right !'

And I rode on, nor know what next bechanced
Till came these five across my path, and joined
Me in the quest ; and all of us pursued
The wandering fires that Guelpho spoke about ;
Nor came we near a chance of ale at all
Till, seeing your sign swinging, we came here ;
And now you baulk our craving."

                  "So I do,"
Said John the Nobbly One ; " and so I must,
Unless you prove you're ' *bony-fidys*,' there."
" Surely," said he that just had told the tale,

" I've travelled far enough to meet the Act,"

" Then where's your ticket ? " asked old Walking-
    shaw.

And he—the knight—not having one, was dumb.

But presently he spoke : " How near," said he,

" Have you a railway-station to your house ? "

" Five miles," said Johnny; and the knight was
    dumb.

" You please *must* go," the Nobbly One went on ;

" The constables is werry 'ard on me ;

To catch you here would mean my licence gone."

In vain the weary ones remonstrated ;

Old Johnny stuck to his original text.

How 'twould have ended, who can think or say ?

But while the argument was at its height

Time hurried on, and, ere the squabble ceased,

The bells chimed merrily the hour of six.

Then all the six fell on each other's necks,

And hastily was broached a cask of ale ;

And when the constable next passed that way,

He took a half-a-crown to keep his gaze

Directed on a neighbouring field ; and so

The "*bony-fidys*" did their best 'gainst time.

But when next he who told the tale did meet

His liege, he murmured, "Guelpho, thou wert

   right!"

SILLEAS AND GETTARRE.

SILLEAS AND GETTARRE.

G AY Guelpho made new knights to fill the gap
Left by the Alpine Club ; and as he sat
One day at home, with weed and wine, the door
Was softly open'd, and through it a youth,
Silleas, and a smell of Jockey Club
Pass'd, and he bore a letter in his hand.

'Twas writ by old Sir Jones for Silleas,
And introduced him to the Coming K——.
So Guelpho took it, broke the seal and read,
And, reading, all his genial features beamed.
" So ho ! so ho ! my youth," thus 'twas he spoke,
" You would be one of us—say, is it so ? "
And Silleas like a maiden flushed, and said,
" I would, O Guelpho, that is my desire :
Make me a knight, because the very thought

Of knighthood thrills ! '' The Coming K—— looked
    grave.

'' It thrills you, does it ?   Ah, that's very bad,
I fear ; '' so Guelpho spoke.   '' You have been led
To read those Idylls, drawn from ancient lore,
That tell of Arthur's knights ? ''   And Silleas
    bowed.

'' That's very bad,'' said Guelpho.   You must know
My knights are of a very different kind.
We don't ride forth redressing wrongs ; we find
It is enough to dress ourselves, young man.
We don't in damp old chapels vigils keep,
Or ride a-tilt, or put on casques or greaves ;
We do not rescue maidens in distress—
Our motives might, you see, be misconstrued.
Mine *have* been, once or twice unpleasantly.
I would not that such trouble came again.
And much more careful am I than I was ;—
One illness and one witness-box's enough.
But 'twas a game of chess ; and some called check,

And check was it, but Castl'ing had just saved me.
You know the formula that reigns in States,
To wit, ' Le roi est mort ; vive le roi.'
Well, though I like a lark like any one—
' Once bit, twice shy '—one thinks unto oneself ;
And a real duffer one would be to play
Into the hands of those who prophesy
That *Vivat Rex* will ne'er our playbills end ;
And last loyal cheer, *Vivat Regina* be.
I say, we cleave not barons to the chine,
Or have at villains in the public ways ;
We do not fight for golden circlets now,—
In short, we don't make asses of ourselves."
To all which Silleas listened in amaze,
And with his feet he fidgeted, and strok'd
All nervously the fluff upon his lips ;
Till, finding presently his voice, he said,
" What must I do, then, to be knight of thine ?"
Then Guelpho bade him sit, and poured him out
A glass of brimming ripe old burgundy,

M

And said, "Well, Silleas, I suppose you smoke?"

But Silleas answered, "Sire, I cannot say

I do, although I own I've tried." At which

The prince his head did shake, and murmured low,

"Ah, much I fear me, he has much to learn."

Then loudly, "Do you know your way about?"

And Silleas flushed again, and shook his head.

"But," said he, "I have bought a guide and map."

At which rejoinder Guelpho fairly yell'd.

"By way about," he said, "I meant to ask

If you were up to all the tricks of town;

Whether you knew the way to go the pace;

The 'O. K.' thing, you know." And Silleas stared;

So blankly stared that Guelpho yelled again,

And said, "Methinks that you are rather green.

Say, have you e'er ta'en supper at Cremorne?

You've not? Nor been at all behind the scenes?

Still no? Come, come, young man, you've much to

   do.

I'll warrant me you're not in debt a bit;

Don't know a pretty horse-breaker, nor make

A book upon the races.　Sir, you must

Reform; you've time and money, go then forth

And win your spurs; then hie you back to me,

When, if you kindly take to our gay life,

I'll dub you of my Dinner Table Knights.

Go forth!"　And with obeisance to his Lord

Did Silleas go forth—in sooth went first.

So this young man, this Silleas of the West—

But lately come to his inheritance—

Walked on and on, till to the Park he came;

Thrice being trodden to his death he 'scaped

By prancing chargers or by restive steeds;

Then, guided by a p'liceman, haven found,

And, panting, rested, leaning on a rail.

There, as he lean'd, he look'd about and saw,

Behind, a roadway wide, of yielding tan;

Before, a carriage road, and it was blocked

With equipages stately by the score.

Near him were mounds of even sloping turf,

Whereon a thousand shrubs and trees did grow ;

Around him beds of rainbow-tinted flowers,

And crowds of folks in rainbow-tinted garb.

Far as his eye could reach were carriages,

And flowers, and pretty girls, and well-dressed men.

The more he looked the more was he entranced

With what he saw on every side of him.

It seemed to him it was another world

From that he'd known at Slushboro'-in-the-Slooze,

So much so that his eyes were dazzled by 't ;

So much so that the swell-mobsman who passed

Played on his mood and eased him of his watch,

Which knowing not, he heeded not, but looked

And longed, and longed and looked again ; till he,

Half dreaming, well nigh nodded o'er the rail,

Closing his eyes in rapturous ecstasy.

Suddenly waken'd by a sound of talk

And laughter underneath his very nose,

He, looking up, glanced o'er the rails, and saw

A damsel clad in colours like the clouds

Of sunset and of sunrise : and she drove

A pair of ponies, ponies richly trapt,

That drew a phaeton of dainty build.

Behind, with liveried coat, cockaded hat,

And faultless tights and boots, a " tiger " sat.

The damsel sat alone, a picture she,

For large her violet eyes look'd, and her bloom

Was well put on ; artistically spread ;

With skilful pencilling were her eyebrows arched ;

Rich was the colour loaded on her lips.

Her hair, save to the roots contiguous,

Where nature did assert herself, all gold ;

Behind, gold all, but that was hairpinn'd on.

Round were her arms, mature in womanhood,

And full her bust—or so at least it seemed—

And slender was her hand that held the reins,

And stout the chain that twined about her neck,

And large her lockets ; grandiose her brooch ;

And bracelets, like to fetters, bound her wrists.

Her clothes were splendid, though a little loud,

Unlike her voice, which was full loud indeed.

There, loitering by the rail, she reined her steeds,

While scented dandies laughed and chaffed with
  her,

And swells, all stick and eye-glass, stopped and
  stared.

She seemed a mimic monarch in her court,

And saucy queendom sat upon her brow.

Then Silleas, when he looked, beheld, and lo!

The beauty of her flesh abashed the boy;

(He knew not Madame Corinne's secrets then),

And open-mouth'd he gazed upon her charms.

P'rhaps rudely, for he recently had come

Far from an uncouth county in the West,

Where, saving his own sisters, he had known

Scarce any but the buxom dairy-maids—

Rough souls, that laugh'd and scream'd against the
  gulls

That flew o'er Slushborough from the sounding sea.
Then with a slow smile look'd the damsel round
Upon her gay admirers ; and as, when
Trodden upon, a worm will slowly turn
Its tail up towards the sun, so turned her nose,
Tip-tilted like a well-worn Balmoral,
Up heavenwards ; for she did despise them all,
Being empty fools.   And she was called Gettarre,
A noted member of the " Hemisphere."

So chanced it that her gaze on Silleas lit,
And something in his honest foolish face,
Which still was fixed on her with rapturous stare,
Did please her fickle fancy for the while ;
And she resolved to have some fun with him.
So, with a nod dismissing all the swells
Who hung about her phaeton, she whipped up
The ponies, reined them in, and dropped her whip,
As though by accident, where Silleas stood.
At first he moved not, and the " tiger " leapt,

Limb-nimble, from his seat to pick it up.
But with her hand his mistress waved him back,
Looked languishing at Silleas with her eyes,
And said, all sweetly, " May I trouble you ? "
Taken aback, he blushed like fire, and stooped,
And clumsily restored the dainty thong.

At which she said, " O most uncouth young man,
Knowest thou not the fashion of our speech ?
Or hast thou but a fair and foolish face,
Lacking a tongue ? "

                        " O damsel," answered he,
(He really did say " ma'am," but what of that ?)
" I am a country youth, and, seeing you,
Was dazzled by the sudden light, and crave
Your pardon."   " It is granted ! " said she then.
" Where go you ?"   And he said, " I do not know."
" Then dive beneath the rail, and by my side
Get in," she said.   And down the Drive they went

'Midst such a crowd and cram of carriages,
It seemed as though Long Acre had turned out
Its stock-in-trade into the teeming Park.
And while they drove, the meaning in his eyes,
His simpleness of manner and chaste awe,
His broken utterances and bashfulness
Began to bore her, till within her heart
She mutter'd, " I have lighted on a fool—
Raw, very raw ! "   But since her mind was bent
Upon another conquest, and she wished
To pique her swell admirers every one,
She smiled upon him and she flatter'd him,
Being so gracious, that he could not make
Out head or tail of it, all was so strange,
But deeper fell and deeper yet in love,
And fancied she loved him.

                              And when they'd driven
All down the Drive to Guelpho Gate and back,
Some twice or thrice, she his hand taking, spoke,

" Now I must say good bye, but don't forget

You've seen Gettarre, thro' swelldom ' Floorer '
    called.

Perchance some day you her again will see :

Say, would you like to ? "

                              Then his smitten heart

Leapt, and he cried " Ay ! " — and the ponies
    jumped—

" Ay, that should I ! " he answered, and she laugh'd

And straightway squeezed his hand, and flung it
    from her.

And he, alighting, caught his foot and fell.

Then, picking up himself, began to muse,

While she, well rid of him, did plume herself ;

Then glanced askew at some gay Guelphic knight,

And, winking wickedly, did pass away.

" O, happy world ! " mused Silleas. " All, meseems,

Are happy ; I the happiest of them all."

Then brushed the gravel from his clothes, and sank
Into a vacant iron chair, with arms.
" She squeezed my hand.   Oh, happy, happy me !
What can I do to show my love for her ?
I'd sacrifice my "—   " Twopence," said a man,
Who paused before him with a courier bag
Slung at his side, and badge upon his cap.
" Twopence ! " cried Silleas.   " Ay ! my life, my all,
I'd give for her ! "   And as he shouted this,
The men who passed him rounded on their heels,
And wonder'd at him ; but the man explained.
So, blushing, Silleas fished two coppers out,
And paid them gladly ; then at rest was he.

Then Guelpho passed on horseback, and he saw
Poor Silleas sitting, and he reined his steed.
" What fare, young man ? " he said, and Silleas
        jumped,
And starting up, said, " I have seen Gettarre ! "
" Floorer ! " said Guelpho.   " Why, that is A 1 ;

You lose no time in looking into life.

Where go you now?"   And Silleas shook his head.

" Then dine with me at eight," said Guelpho,

   "sharp;"

Pricked then his steed, and caracoled away.

So Guelpho dined, and Silleas was there,

With Loosealot, Heraint, and many more

Such Dinner-Table Knights; and there was served

All that was choice from air, land, stream, and sea,

And Silleas proved a valiant trencherman.

Then, after ruddy wine and brown cigars

Had made the circuit of the table square,

Did Guelpho, bearing his new guest in mind,

Propose for him a spree to end the night;

So whispered he to Loosealot, who rose,

And, taking Silleas by his willing arm,

Led him far out into the noisy night,

And, hailing cab, did drive to Windmill Street.

Then rang the sound of music on their ears;

Then roared the rout of revelry; the heat

Came eddying down the glittering corridors;

But, heeding not, they laid down coins and
    passed

Where folly smiled at beauty; beauty, too,

Not to be outdone, did at folly wink;

Where all above was firmament of gas;

Where all the walls were mirrors, and the seats

Velvet; the gilded gallery was crown'd

With faces; and the great hall filled with folk

From end to end; and played the orchestra

The valse, quadrille, and galop; and some danced,

While others at side buffets, full of glass,

Of glitter and of glare, did stand and suck

Iced sweetnesses through lengths of rustic reed,

Or mixed the tawny port with lemonade;

Or smacked their painted lips o'er rich liqueurs;

Others, again, did walk and chaff, and talk

With gestures manifold, and archness marked;

And all the women were in gay attire,
All merry with a forced merriment.

Then blew the cornet and the fiddlers tweaked,
And blithely flew the dancers o'er the floor;
Silleas was much impress'd at it; his eyes
Sparkled; he caught Sir Loosealot by the arm.
" O what and where is this," he cried, " Sir
    Knight ?"
Said Loosealot, " This is but a phase of life;
See to it, I must leave you now.   Ta-ta!
Beware the paint !"   And with these words he left.

Then did the helpless heart of Silleas fail,
And, looking round, he shook upon his feet—
For he had smoked cigars of flavour full,
He, custom'd, heretofore, to nought but cane.
What could he do, so bilious and alone ?
The very thought was matchless misery.
But as he looked, all anxious, it so chanced,

His eye fell on a face he knew: 'twas hers,

Gettarre's, and all his hope revived.

She was the centre of a glowing group

Of white-tied men and rainbow-tinted girls,

And saw not Silleas; but he, recking nought,

Strode to the spot where stood she, and exclaimed,

" O, damsel, see, I look on you again,

I, Silleas of the West ! "   She turned, and said,

" What nonsense is it this rude person talks ?

Speak when you're spoken to !" whereat he jumped

As one who treads upon a carpet-tack,

Glanced once at her, then turned, and blew his nose.

But after, when the final valse was played,

And all the host went crowding to the street,

And she, and those with her, amongst the rest,

Then Silleas followed, and he saw her go

To where a building rose into the night,

Glaring with gas at every window-pane ;

And down below, the folk who passed could see

A store of " natives," and a hoard of prawns ;
A wealth of lobsters, and a stock of crabs—
A pile of piscicultural lavishness ;
All flanked and hemmed about with potted meats,
With sauce in bottles, and sardines in tins ;
And crown'd with lettuce green, and endive crisp,
And samphire, smelling of the sounding sea.
Here they went in, and Silleas saw them pass
Away, and then ascend a winding stair ;
Stood he all melancholy, there outside,
Leaning all pensive on a pillar-box.

From this vantage viewed he his lady fair
Sit by the window on the first-floor front,
And watched her carefully, and saw them bring
To her and hers of plates that hissed and steam'd ;
Of bottles, too, with foil upon the corks,
That loudly popped and beaded in the glass.
So kept he watch and ward ; and many passed
And chaffed him on his miserable mood ;

Offered to stand him supper, and the like.

But Silleas persevered, nor heeded them.

At last, o'ercome with heat, the fair Gettarre

Flung up the window close to which she sat,

And, looking out, she saw him ; and she cried,

"There is that fool again," and motioned him

To pass away ; but Silleas sighed and stayed.

And this persistence turn'd her scorn to wrath ;

Then calling on the swells, she charged them, "Out !

And drive that muff away."   And out they came,

And swaggered up to him, and shook their fists,

And said, "Be off with you !"   But Silleas, brave

In his wrapt love, would not be off ; but stayed,

And all the three defied.   So these returned,

But still he lean'd upon the pillar-box.

Thereon her wrath became a hate ; and once

Again she cried, "Out ! and away with him !

Look at the man ; he haunts, besieges me.

Down ! strike him ! get him locked up ! anything

N

To drive him from my sight." And down they went,

And, warm with wine, squared up to Silleas.

But Silleas overthrew them one by one ;

And from the first-floor window cried Gettarre,

" Be off with you," and pelted him with corks,.

And bits of lobster-shell.   Then, the police,

When all was over, with a rush, came up,

And, seeing Silleas with bleeding nose,

A battered " Lincoln," and a tattered coat,

And noting furthermore he now was weak,

They captured him, and straightway ran him in.

With headache terrible he did next day

Before a magistrate appear, and paid

A penalty for all that he had done ;

Then hied to Guelpho, and revealed his tale.

" So, ho !" quoth merrily the Coming K——,

" You quickly learn the mysteries of life ;

Go on as you've begun, and soon, ay, soon

You shall be knight of mine, my beamish boy !"

Yet Silleas felt sorrow, for he loved

Gettarre most fondly, 'spite what she had done ;

So prowled he ever looking after her,

That he might tell her how he loved her still.

To find her, he would don his gloves, and pace

The pavement of the Burlington Arcade,

Where, either side of him, were windows piled

With all the lavish aids of luxury,

Ingenious in utter uselessness.

To find her out, he sought the lamp-lit groves

Of Chelsea's Gardens, Canon-curst Cremorne,

Roamed there amidst the plaster images,

List to the band, and sat the ballet out.

To see her face, he braved the Surrey-side,

Its gardens haunted, sailed upon the lake,

Saw Blondin walk, the final rocket fired,

Then languished listlessly back to his bed.

The theatres all knew him, and the Halls,

Where " comiques " reign and cads are reckoned

    " stars."

He ranged the " Zoo " on Sunday, oft dropped in
At the Alhambra for a minute's space ;
Went here, there, everywhere to find his love ;
Yet found her not ; but all the while he grew
In knightly knowledge, and for Guelpho fit.

One day, as close to Leicester Square he passed,
Bound upon solitary search, he met
An open-faced and merry-seeming man,
Who, stopping, said, " Hail ! whosoe'er thou art,
I like thy look, thou'rt after my own mind.
Where goest thou ? "   And Silleas replied,
How he his spurs was winning ; how he sought
To learn his way about, and go the pace,
And fit himself, indeed, for Guelpho's knight.
Then said the stranger, " True, thou art in luck,
For I will be thy guide, and act thy friend ;
I know my way about ; I'll show it thee ;
And by my help thou shalt go quite the pace."
So Silleas, still so green, and far from sharp,

The stranger welcomed with an open heart,
And made him from that hour his guide and friend.
So Swindlain—thus the stranger's name was called—
Took Silleas in hand and bore his purse,
And taught him how to know his way about,
And how to go the pace.   And Silleas found
It was expensive work ; but little cared
How much he lost at billiards or at bowls,
Or how his wine-bill waxed, or how it was
That Swindlain never paid for anything ;
Enough for him that he was seeing life.
And so he went upon the turf and bought
A book metallic for his bets, and backed
The Coming K——'s mare, Goanveer, to win
A sum quite fabulous at heavy odds.
He went behind the scenes and saw strange sights,
Comedians drinking stout like other men,
Tragedians playing cards, and ballet-girls
Nursing their babies in between the acts.
He joined a club, which, six months later on,

Wound up, and let him in for scores of pounds;

He learned to draw a bill, to fly a kite,

And build up credit with thin paper bricks;

He learned to smoke without a Nemesis

Of giddy headache following him next day;

He got to know the names of wines, and talked

Of fruity ports and Piper's *Sec* champagne;

He horses kept at livery—in sooth,

He kept a stud, to judge by what they cost;

He dined, danced, dissipated, drawled,

And passed, in short, for quite a modern knight.

But all this time he ne'er had seen Gettarre,

Though still he loved her dearly through it all,

And yearned for her.   So said he on a time,

" Swindlain, I love a lady and she's lost;"

Then told him all the tale of his fond love.

And Swindlain answer'd kindly, tho' in scorn,

" Is that all, Silleas?   Then may you cheer up;

Methinks I know this 'Floorer' by repute.

Come, trust in me ; hereby I pledge my troth ;

Yea, by the honour of a dinner knight,

I will find out your loved one, and subdue

Her scornful nature to your ardent love.

Lend me your purse, give me some blank cheques
    signed,

And I will seek thy irate damsel out ;

Will tell her you are dead, that she may then

Invite me in to tell about your death.

Then, when I come within her counsels, then,

From breakfast-time to grog-time I will chant

Your praise as truest lover and best knight ;

I'll sound your praises, till she fain shall long

To have you back in lusty life again,

To love thee. Wherefore now thy horse

And cheque-book ; let me go ; be comforted.

Give me three days to meet her fancy shape ;

The third night hence will bring you news of her.

Meanwhile, look at the *Telegraph's* back page,

And there you'll see what news I have to tell."

Then Silleas gave his cheque-book and his purse
To Swindlain, saying, " Betray me not, but help,
Nor prove thyself to be but light of love."
" Ay ! " said Swindlain, " ay, trust me, Silleas ; "
Then bounded from him, his umbrella raised,
And brought a hansom dashing to the curb ;
Then, whispering " Fulham Road," he drove away,
A corner turned, and then no more was seen.

When blush'd and broke the morning following this
Sat Silleas toying with his toast ; and he
Sent out a trusty messenger, who brought,
Wet from the press, a *Daily Telegraph,*
And, turning to its column ultimate,
He found a mystic notice worded thus :—
" Swindlain to Silleas.—I have found her out ;
She lives at Fulham ; all will yet be well."
And Silleas was glad, and cracked an egg,
And took more coffee on the strength of it.
So three days passed, and, loitering aimlessly,

Did Silleas kick his heels about the town.

Then, when the next one dawned with no fresh
    news,

He waxed incontinent, and used bad words.

Another passed, and yet no Swindlain came ;

But came a letter telling Silleas how

Large cheques had been presented at his bank,

Which, signed by him, his balance had o'erdrawn.

Then Silleas rose up, his bootlace girt,

And went to find his false and faithless friend.

The night was hot ; he could not rest ; but drove

To Brompton Road, and then dismissed the cab,

And wandered into Fulham, wearily,

To seek Gettarre and find the base Swindlain.

He asked for her at bakers' shops ; but none

Was there that knew a lady of that name.

Of hurrying postmen asked he for Gettarre ;

And they replied, " But what's her other name ? "

He none but " Floorer " knew.   So he passed on.

And midnight came, and still he searched for her.

To tell the knockers that he knocked, the bells
He pulled, the servants brought he to the door,
Would be to furnish forth a catalogue
More tedious far than Homer's " List of Ships."
At last, he chanced upon a road that left
The highway, sloping to the river broad,
A road retired and rural, with a row
Of trees adown it—high were they, and elms;
On each side, villas with small lawns in front;
And fate led Silleas that road to try.

House after house he passed, and all was still,
Till one he came to with an open gate
And lighted window.   Up to it he went;
And heard but his own steps, and his own heart
Beating, for he was trespassing he knew.
Still on he went across the little lawn
Unto the front door; that was fastened, though;
Then was he 'ware that all the blinds were up,
And from behind a lilac-bush he look'd

Into the room that ope'd upon the lawn,

And saw—the woman he had come to seek,

And with her the base Swindlain, light of love.

Back as a hand that takes a maiden's waist

And finds a pin run into it, he drew ;

Back as the public which expects Sims Reeves

Go, when they read the tenor's taken ill ;

Or as a man retreats from mud-cart's spoon ;

Did Silleas, overcome with feeling, start.

But curiosity o'ercame disgust :

'Tis often so : and he crept back again,

And from the lilac had another look.

He saw a supper-table spread for two,

With dainties lavish, and with wines profuse,

Remains of salad ; where the lobster flesh

Gleamed white as snow on Mount Soracte's head,

The board bestrewed ; and there were chickens'
    limbs,

And pigeon-pie, and *pâtés de foie gras.*

But who shall tell the wealth of wine had flowed ?

Ah, who indeed ? and Echo answers, " Who ? "

For Silleas, though a novice in such things,

Saw on the table costly vintages,

And writhed to think his money paid for them.

And there sat Swindlain, all the worse of wine,

His neck-tie bow beneath his sin'ster ear,

His hair all ruffled, and his front all creased,

His hiccough sounding in the silent air,

And by his side, Gettarre, all flushed did sit,

And stirred her wine up with a lobster-claw,

All lovely looked she, saving that her eyes

Were wild and blood-shot, and her nose all red ;

And as poor Silleas watched, she fell asleep,

Her head on Swindlain's shoulder ; who himself

Likewise succumbed, and both began to snore.

Then Silleas crept yet nearer to the house,

And found the window opened at his touch ;

So, fingering where his sword-blade would have
    been,

Had it been that he carried one, he said,

" I will go in and slay them where they sleep."

But as he thought awhile, he changed his mind,

For he remembered that the law was strict,

That those brave knights who slew their foes, or

    fought

For innocence, might haply catch it hot,

Should they be caught and brought before a beak.

So, thinking all this over, he exclaimed,

" What, slay a sleeping knight ?   This must not be.

He's false, and she is false, but let that pass."

So he stepped gingerly into the room

And into Swindlain's pockets poured champagne,

And filled them up with filbert-shells, and placed

Fragments of chicken-bone in both his boots ;

Then with a knife cut off his left moustache,

And rubbed his heavy head with bloater paste ;

Then tied his coat-tail to the bell-rope, and

Unhitched Gettarre's profusion of false hair,

And satisfied himself her teeth were false,

Her bosom padded, and her face got up ;

Then turn'd, and so return'd, and, laughing, tied
A napkin round each of their naked necks,
And, emptying all the wine about the floor,
He took his card, with " P. P. C." writ on,
And placed it on the table prominent ;
Then left them snoring, in a thorough draught.

And forth he passed, and made for his own home,
And felt his silly love for her was gone;
Nor did he for the moment recollect
How both of them had made him such a fool ;
But comforted himself with his revenge,
Which shows how much like other men he was.

Then she that felt the cold air of the night
Playing about her almost unthatched poll
Awoke, and turn'd herself, and, seeing him
A sight most ludicrous, did yell with mirth ;
At which he, starting up, the bell-rope tugged
Unconsciously; and all the servants came,

And, seeing such a pair of objects, shrieked
With laughter; and Gettarre thus spake
To Swindlain, "Liar! Silleas is not dead;
Here he has been to-night; for see his card,
And trace around his fanciful conceits.
So get thee gone!" And he that tells the tale
Says that her ever-veering fancy turn'd
To Silleas as the one true man on earth
She wished to love her, and in great despair
She went into a Refuge, and there died.

But he made still for home. But cabs were not,
And so he walked until the daylight dawned,
Till, by fatigue o'ercome, he almost dropped,
But reached at last his destined lodging-place;
Then, sleeping long and soundly, he arose,
And once more sought and saw the coming K——,
And said, "Oh, Guelpho, take me for a knight,
For now I know my way about a bit;
I'm now well up in all the tricks of town;

I know likewise the way to go the pace."

Then Guelpho answer'd, " If this should be so,

You shall be one of us at once, sweet youth.

But tell me what you've done, and where you've
     been."

Then Silleas spoke, and told to Guelpho all—

How he had loved Gettarre, now her did hate ;

How he had met Swindlain, who cheated him ;

How he had run up bills, and been " run in."

In short, did tell him such a parlous tale

Of deeds of gallantry and folly done,

Of weaknesses displayed, and slangy acts,

That Guelpho took him warmly to his arms,

And dubbed him knight that moment with his sword.

Henceforward Silleas deserved the name,

For he was fastest of the company,

And did much honour to the dinner things ;

Till, running through his property at last,

He died a pauper at an early age.

THE LAST CARNIVAL.

THE LAST CARNIVAL.

BAGONET the fool, whom Guelpho in his moods
Had made one of his famous Table Knights,
At Pimlico, high on the second floor,
Danced like a lunatic before his glass.
Toward him, from Bow Street Station, all unshav'd,
And, knocking at his door peremptorily,
Came Criscram, saying, "Are you in, old muff?"
For Guelpho and Sir Loosealot, straying once
About the occidental end of town,
Entered by chance a Music Hall. It reeked
With bad tobacco, and with yet worse fumes
Of alcohol; but full was it, forsooth,
And on the stage a "Lion Comique" sang
Some lay that dealt of Charles, nicknamed "Cham-
    pagne,"
Which Guelpho pleased; as did the following song

Of " Roaring Rams." And said the Coming K——,
" O, Loosealot, this minstrel pleases me ;
I'd hear again this merry troubadour."
To whom Sir L. : " Then let it be so, liege,"
And gave he orders, and the thing was done.

So came the " Jolly Cad," for it was he—
He came and sang in Guelpho's Royal Halls ;
Earned his approval, and was henceforth known
As he who'd sung before the Coming K——.
And Guelpho liked his drolleries right well.
But came a time—this was before the race,
When the fell trick of Loosealot came out—
That Guelpho long'd for something to dispel
The anxious feeling bred of Goanveer,
Who, ever present in his thoughts, became
A bore by day, a nightmare when he slept ;
So gave command that there should forthwith
    be
A comic carnival, and named the day,

And bid his Knights attend him ; and they came,
Prepar'd for revel with their Coming K——.

Came Loosealot—round whose sick head all night
Wet towels had been enwrapt—he'd left awhile
The tending of his Goanveer ; and came
Uxorious Heraint ; Silleas, the fool ;
Pert Vilien, and Coachington the gay ;
And Northerland, the lord of many isles ;
Came, too, the young De Bauch ; and Camelot's
    Earl,
Who had but lately come from Southern seas ;
And Badminton, from Lyonesse, and all
The nameless women who had fame, and all
The flower of Guelpho's younger Knights ; and lo !
Last, and not least, came Guelpho in himself.

He glanced and saw the goodly company
Of noble men and noted women there ;
With cheerful greetings welcomed all, and then

Ascending, filled his favourite easy-chair,

Facile princeps, looking over all,

And said, " O, Knights and ladies, this is well ;

Bid now the comic carnival commence ! "

Then came the singers of the Music Halls,

And first to come was Baggs, called the " Immense,"

A little man, but, O ! a mighty Cad ;

And sang he lyrics of the present day,—

Of " Sweet Jemimar," who liv'd in Shoreditch,

And sold eel-pies and " trotters " of the sheep ;

Of how he'd met upon a Penny Boat,

The relict of the late lamented Jones,

Who, giving him her olive-branch to hold,

Had left him with it at the Nine Elms Pier ;

Of " 'Andsome Sam," the beau-ideal of men,

Who " rollicked " every night, whate'er that means,

Insulted every one he met, and reach'd

His home each morning with the " Simpson'd "
        milk ;

Which songs were loudly cheer'd, as though they'd
    been
The witty labour of a clever man.
Then came the " Lion Comique," a greater cad,
If might be, than the Baggs they called " Immense ; "
He sang, too, choice selections from *his* store,
Stuff'd full of slang, and dirty every one.
He dressed in velvet coats and flaring " pants,"
In sham seal waistcoats, and in neckties loud,
And he was cheer'd, and then he passed in turn ;
And came the " Jolly Cad," long-looked-for, last.
He sang his latest triumphs ; sang he then
Of how he lived on champagne and cigars :
Detailed his East-end amours, and enlarg'd
On all that's most contemptible in man.
And, as he sang, a gray-haired courtier passed,
Who'd been a man when Guelpho was a boy,
And to his ears sounded as in a dream
The shameless singing of that arrant cad.
And look'd he in at open door, and stay'd

Gloomily, sighing wearily as one

Who stands and gazes on a faded fire

When all the goodlier guests are passed away;

And, as he look'd, he heard the voices roar

An ocean-sounding welcome to the cad,

Until he groan'd for wrath to see the sight,

To hear the sound, and moaned, " O, crying shame;

The glory of our knighthood is no more!"

But knew not Guelpho was so soon to be

Purged as by fire, and made thenceforth more meet.

So knight and damsel joined the Jolly Cad

In chorus; and the beading glass went round;

And Guelpho took his finger-circlet off,

And put it on the Jolly Cad's black hand.

And still the ancient courtier look'd, and said,

" Shade of South Kensington! what's this I see?

Better thy scientific craze by far,

Thy model dairies and thy puffy pigs,

Thy love of tin-mining in Cornish land,

Thy love for art, and what Art Buildings bring;

Better King Cole and all his artful courts,

Than orgies such as these ! "   And so he passed,

Nor knew that Guelpho yet would much amend.

Then wax'd the revelry and waned the sense

Of those who joined in it, and the wan night

Went glooming out, and dawn'd another day ;

And still did Guelpho's carnival go on.

So knight and damsel glitter'd at the feast

Variously gay : for he that tells the tale

Was there to see, and wondered at the sight—

The roystering revels and the mirth so loud,

The boisterous doings at those lawless jousts.

Then passed the brimming bowl, and passed the
     jest,

And told the Dinner-Table Knights, their deeds,

Told he that Camelot's earldom held, the tale

Of all his travels in the Southern Isles

With one who bears a literary name ;

Not reverently, but flippantly, he told

The things that chanced them there, nor cared one
    whit
That much he said would bring the blush of grief
Upon his mother's face, could she have heard.
And told young Coachington of prowess done:
How he had knock'd an old man's hat well off,
And answered for it 'fore a magistrate ;
How he had driven a coach-and-four for hire ;
And loud they cheer'd this chivalry confess'd.
Nor held the Coming K—— his peace, but told
How he had gained his knighthood and his name ;
How he had follow'd pleasure ; oft pursued
Here, there, and everywhere, his senses, tastes,
And appetites ; and happy, tight, he hoped
They all might be.

               Did boast his trusty Knights
Their deeds of knightly kind ; nor did conceal
What 'twas of which true knighthood was com-
    pos'd ;

Whence he who tells the tale did come to know

A modern knight's chief qualities are these :—

He must be able liquors to imbibe

Of many quantities ; nor must he fail

To be a valiant trencherman ; and he

Must be well up in knightly slang and chaff,

And own that parents now are quite play'd out.

Marriage he must eschew ; but still maintain

Expensive villas in the Fulham Road,

Or in the " Wood." His tradesmen rarely pay ;

" Whitewash " regard as patent of his rank ;

Some time or other he must hope to lease

A theatre ; must have an interest

In each big race, or make a book on it ;

Smoke like a furnace ; gamble, if needs be ;

Know all the dyed-haired, painted queans who leer

Upon the stage or from the window-pane ;

Shoot, when he's called upon, the pheasants tame

That hover round his gun ; or e'en despatch

A timid pigeon flying from a trap.

Moreover, he must make inane remarks;
Be bored at everything; affect a lisp;
Profess he's steeped with silly cynicism;
And ever try to hide what brain he has,
And never once pronounce the letter " R."
Still further, he must dress himself as though
He were a tailor's dummy, not a man;
Make grooms his confidants, blacklegs his friends,
And stifle all that's noble in his heart.
Then—if the one who heard the tale tells right—
He is a model Dinner-Table Knight!

Meanwhile the carnival had worn away;
The sports broke up, and slowly reeled the guests;
Some to their homes, in friendly hansom borne;
Some, riotous, to p'lice-cells proximate,
Where, passing, all unconsciously, some noisy
          hours,
At length were charged, were fin'd, did pay, and
          passed.

'Mongst these was Criscram, who, in joyous mood,

Had kicked a peeler and put out a lamp.

And little Bagonet (as before was said),

High up in his back rooms in Pimlico,

Danced like a lunatic before his glass.

Then Criscram, saying, "Are you in, old muff?"

Wheel'd round on either heel. Bagonet replied,

"Ay, ay, come in!" And Criscram came, and said,

"Why skip ye so, Sir Fool?" And Bagonet:

"Because I've made a riddle." Criscram: "What?"

The other: "Listen, and you it shall hear.

Why is the tool you have not used to-day

Upon your chin, when 'tis with ink besmear'd,

Like that knife, ace-of-spade shaped, which they use

To scratch out blots?" and Criscram shook his
    head.

And Bagonet, still skipping: "Will you give

It up?" And Criscram: "Yes, I will." Then he

Who made it answered it and said, "Because

It is an inky razor ; "* and he skipp'd amain.
"Sir Fool," said Criscram, " I will break your head
If you repeat an outrage such as this.
I did not come for riddles ; I have come
Straight from the Police Court to avail myself
Of these thy rooms ; I want to dress myself
Without going home to Finchley."   " Dress away,"
Said Bagonet.   So Criscram dress'd away,
Wash'd, shav'd himself, and brush'd his hair,
And wiped the mud off his bespattered clothes.
Then, as he waited for his polished boots,
He sang to Bagonet, and this he sang :

" Free love—cries Woodhull—love but while you may;
   Don't try to love one wife for evermore ;
Love fades and dies, the yearning goes away ;
   New love, new wife—what matter if a score ?
New wife, new love to suit the newer day :
   New wives are sweet as those that went before.

---

* Ink eraser.—*He that tells the tale.*

Free love—says Woodhull—love but while you
    may."

And Bagonet listen'd, with his foot in hand,

Hopping about the room, and then replied,

" Friend, what is this you mean, I do not see ;

Are you about to sail for Brigham Young

And write a book, like Necworth Nickson did ?"

But Criscram : " Pish !" and " Psha ! You are a
    fool !

For I have flung thee pearls and find thee swine."

And Bagonet, turning on his foot's ball,

And pausing in his Can-can with the chair :

" Dost know the difference, Criscram, my friend,

Between our Guelpho and the ocean's froth ?

I tell thee, though I am put down as fool,

The one's the Coming K——, the other's scum."*

And Criscram : " Ay, Sir Fool, the Coming K——

Went it last night." And Bagonet replied,

---

* The other's come.—*He that tells the tale.*

" Tuwhoo ! do ye see it ? do ye see the star ? "

And skipp'd more urgently about the room.

" Nay, fool," said Criscram, " for I will not look,

Since stars shine not in sunny mid-day hour."

" Well, I can see it," said the fool, " and so

Can Guelpho, that is why I skip so much."

And Criscram : " Treason, Bagonet, you talk,

To call the Coming K—— a brother fool."

Then Bagonet clear'd the table at a bound,

And jump'd successively o'er all his chairs.

" Ay, ay, my brother fool, tip-top of fools !

What ! could he think, O Criscram, he might sow

Wild oats, and yet reap wheat, neglect the land,

And hope a prosp'rous rule ; and make his Knights

Respected, though they one and all are fools ? "

And, throwing at him all the books that lay

Within his reach, did Criscram pass downstairs ;

And Bagonet resum'd his skipping till

The lodger on the floor below came up,

And said he'd kill him if he skipt ; and so
He skapt no more, but play'd the violin.

Now what this interview between the fool
And Criscram means, or wherefore it is writ,
The one who tells the tale knows not, but as
'Tis written, 'tis as well that it should stand.

And Criscram, thinking of the riddles asked,
Intending to produce them as his own,
Walked musing slowly to Victoria,
Where, taking train, he rode toward the West ;
And as he went he thought upon the maid
He'd vowed to marry in the Finchley road ;
But he was bound to see another girl,
His last attraction, homing at the time
 Neath the escutcheon of a brother Knight,
Sir Luke, a fact which Criscram knew full well.
And she, tiring of him, and fancying
That Criscram's purse was deeper far than his,

Encouraged her new lover; her address

Gave him; and so he made for Phryne Square,

A stuccoed forest for soiled doves like her

To hide in.

                In a ground-floor window sat,

A Chelsea sunset glorying round her hair,

And stamping palpably what of 't was false,

With carmine on her cheeks, Ida the Quean,

And, when she heard the feet of Criscram grind

The gravel path that led up from the gate,

Jumped up and met him at the door herself

(As 'twas not wise to let the servant see),

And said, " H-s-s-h ! Criscram ; softly tread, for fear

You're heard ! "   So cat-like went they in and sat.

Then she, being worldly-wise, said, " O, sweet Sir,

I feared you were not coming ; you are late."

Then he, great hero that he was, replied,

And told her of his chivalrous address ;

How he had kick'd the p'liceman and destroyed

The lamp, and spent the night in "quod"; and
    she,
Still artful, praised him for his knightly pluck,
And said, "Ah, Luke has never done like thee."
So Criscram flush'd with pride and leered on
    her.

And she, playing with Criscram as a boy
Plays with a May-bug on a pin, spake thus:
"O p'liceman-kicker! smasher, too, of lamps!
I am afraid of you, indeed I am.
How could you settle down to household joys?
Perchance you'd want to have a kick at me.
And tell me, too, and tell me true, Lord Knight,
What dame or damsel have ye kneeled to last?"

And Criscram, thinking of the Finchley Road,
"To none, sweet Ida, but I kneel to thee!"
And would have knelt, but feared to bag thereby
His trousers' knee.

And Ida gaily laugh'd.

" Flatter me not," she said, " but tell me what—
What's this 'bout Goanveer and Loosealot ?
Will Goanveer win ?   Is Loosealot a man
Of honour ?   Will you take me to the race ?"

He answer'd, " Certainly, and in your name
I'll put a pony on fleet Goanveer.
Let Loosealot be treach'rous if he dare,
Then must he brave the Coming K———'s great ire,
And we will lynch him as a welsher, dear."

Then Ida, ever dallying with his hand,
Said, " Do you think you love me very much ?
I have expensive tastes, you know, and like
To have what I desire.   Shall it be so ?"
" It shall," said Criscram, " ay, indeed it shall."
" Suppose," said she, " I asked a sealskin coat,
With otter trimmed ?"   Said he : " It should be
    thine."

" And if a hat a week, a dress a month ? "

" They should be thine," he said, and kissed her hand.

Which anger'd her, and she drew back, and said,

" How dare you ? " (Thus she played her little fish.)

Then Criscram moodily paced up and down.

" How dare I, Ida ?   Why, how cross you are!

I've come all this long way to call on you ;

I've promised you all things that you desire,

And yet you will not let me kiss your hand."

So she : " Exactly, you have promised me ;

But what are promises ?   Do you perform ?

How know I that you'll do what you have said ?

You're one of Guelpho's knights—your word means

    nought,

As like as not."

            He, even while she spake,

Mindful of what he'd brought to adorn her with—

The jewels—took out the bracelets from their case,

And clasp'd them both around her shapely wrists ;

Then, pressing closer and still closer, said,

" Now am I trusted ? "   And she, nimble-eyed,

Seeing the stones were good, the gold hall-marked,

Said, " Yes," and did decant some fiery port.

So, then, now she was brought to full accord,

Drank toasts with him, and let him kiss her hand,

And took his ring and placed it on her thumb,

And showed her confidence in such like ways.

Moreover, the piano ope'd and played,

And Criscram, gay, extemporised and sang :

" Ay, ay, O ay, three ays in all you see !

   A star in heaven, a star on earth no more ;

Ay, ay, O ay, whatever ay may be,

   It sounds more fit for ocean than for shore.

Ay, ay, O ay, is what the Jack tars cry,

   As to obey the captain's word they run ;

Ay, ay, O ay—what! three more ays ?   It is

  A fav'rite word in song Arthurian."

Then, by the light's last glimmer, Ida sat

And humbugged Criscram ; and his heart was glad,

For she worked on his fancy dext'rously

Till he had lent her his gold hunter watch ;

Then, when he thought not of it, said to him,

" You'd better go, and come another day ;

If Luke should come, there'd be an awful row."

He rose, he turn'd, and flinging round her neck

His arms, kiss'd her ; but, ere he'd done so twice,

Out of the dark, just as their lips had touched,

Behind him rose a shadow and a cry.

" This is Luke's way," said Luke, and kicked him

    out

Into the passage, and all down the steps,

Until he came to rest upon the curb ;

And, by a p'liceman found, was taken home,

And never went to Phryne Square again,

Or ever saw his watch and ring again.

And he that tells the tale says afterwards

His fancy turned to Finchley Road again ;

But being by her he'd jilted then refused,

A widow married, and has rued the deed.

That night when Criscram came to utter grief

At Phryne Square, did Guelpho, with heartburn

From the effects of yesternight's full cups,

Climb early up the stairway to his couch,

And lay his hot brow on the costly lace,

And said, " Never no more, if I know it ! "

And he did not.   Full ripeness had not come

Yet to his resolution.   But it came.

GOANVEER.

GOANVEER.

FLEET Goanveer had lost the race, and stood
There in the stable near to Epsom Downs,
Neighing; none with her, save a stable lad—
A 'cute one; and he whistled through his teeth
His mem'ries of the songs of music halls;
And jingled in his hands a snaffle-bit,
And winked instinctively; and now and then
Said, "Sanguinary combats, here's a go!"
While Goanveer pricked up her ears and pawed the
    ground.

For hither they had brought her on the day
She lost the Derby: most ill-omened day!
Her jock just saved her from the vengeful crowd,
And here, to safe asylum, smuggled her.

For thus it chanced, one week before the race

She was first fav'rite : betting two to one

Upon her ; and with vote unanimous

The tipsters "Went for her" in all the prints.

It was a "moral" she would win, they said,

And set her name in Roman capitals.

So Guelpho's mare was held in high renown.

Guelpho himself put perfect trust in her,

Believed in Goanveer implicitly,

Nor listened to a breath against her fame ;

But, much embarrassed then by public care,

Had left her mainly in Sir Loosealot's hands ;

For Loosealot always had a horsey turn,

From boyhood had been customed to the turf.

So did the Coming K—— his Loosealot call

And state the case frankly and openly.

"Loosealot !" he said, "of all our Knights most

    fly,

I have a two-year-old : you know her well ;

One of our Royal yearlings was she bred,

And, strange to say, she promised from the first
To be right fast, and so I bought her in—
By friends advised ; have kept her until now.
So far she's ' dark,' but now has come the time
When she must show what she has got in her.
Take her for me, look after her, and see
No harm betides her, and no mischiefs hap ;
See to her training, spare nor time nor coin,
To make her fit for Epsom's course next spring."

" Our mightiest ! " answer'd Loosealot, with a bow,
" O Guelpho, if you thus should honour me,
Sacred will be your trust ! "   (Nor did his words
Tell of the hidden treach'ry of his heart.)

To whom the Coming K——: " Well, take her, then,
And enter her at once at Weatherby's.
She'll win, I'm sure of that, so I'll accept
Long odds about her while I may, and back
Her for such sums as bookmakers will lay."

So Loosealot took her, and he compass'd her

About with seeming kind observances ;

Saw to her training and her exercise,

And busied much himself about her state.

But all the while lurk'd treachery in his soul ;

For he, 'neath open front and pleasant smile,

Conceal'd the grudge he bore the Coming K—— ;

A grudge by woman caused ; hence dire and deep

As all the grudges caused by women are.

What 'twas, the poet will not stay to sing,

An escapade—not more—of Courtly fun,

In which but second fiddle Loosealot played.

And he the Guelpho never had forgiven,

But, seeming friendly, nursed his little wrong

Until it grew, waxèd, and so increased,

It called for some most terrible revenge.

So to his heart low and his breast, he said,

" My time has come ! I'll strike through Goanveer."

The odds, which for a space were very great

'Gainst Goanveer, grew smaller by degrees ;

For it was noised about—how, who can tell ?—

That she, though "dark," was sound and fleet of
     hoof.

But Guelpho, through his agents, at the first,

Booked many bets at forty-five to one

Against his mare, and stood to win a pot

Of money, if she turned out trumps at last.

So passed the months till winter warmed to spring.

And when the daisy all the turf bestarred,

And trees put on their livery of leaves,

Came touts and tipsters to the stable where,

All watched and guarded, Goanveer was kept ;

And, as became their underhanded trade,

They pumped the stable-boys and bribed the grooms,

Climb'd the high tops of boundary-walls, and spied

The mare at exercise ; made mental mems,

And sent their training notes to sporting prints

Of what they'd seen and heard, and much beside.

And—for it suited Loosealot's game—'twas passed

From one to other that the mare was "right."

So, while as yet the cuckoo was not heard,

Evens were offered on her; taken too;

But all the time did Loosealot's revenge

Rankle within him, ruffle all his heart,

As the sharp wind that ruffles all day long

The Channel waves, and passengers makes sick.

And Guelpho, as the time drew near at hand,

Waxed anxious, and foreboding filled his soul.

As day by day his mare went up and up

In public favour, he grew more alarmed;

Would question Loosealot narrowly, and say,

"How goes the mare?" and Loosealot, "All
　　serene!"

Still in the night would visions come to him;

In the dead night grim faces came and went;

And so he dreamed: that he did seem to stand

On some vast plain before a setting sun,

And twenty horses stood in one long row,

While each one lifted up its off front hoof,

And made rude gestures at the sinking orb.
And of the score the foremost was his mare,
Who, when the sun replied with searching glance,
Turned but one somersault, and dropped down fried.
This vision troubled him so much, he said,
" O, Loosealot! look yet closer after her;
For if she wins I am a millionaire—
No bailiffs need I dread, no tradesmen fear;
But if she loses, who will pay my bets ?"
Then Loosealot chuckled inwardly, and went
And laid, by proxy, bets 'gainst Goanveer.

Sped on the weeks, and came the he-cuckoo
To moan monotonous upon the lea;
And came the long-expected Derby week,
And on the mare odds—two to one—were laid;
Came, too, the night before the Derby Day.
To Goanveer it came, and found her fit.
All anxious posted down the Coming K——,
To see his favourite, to pat her neck,

And then to dream of triumph all the night :
But Guelpho knew not all.

                          And Loosealot

Slept not ; but when the darkness, like a pall,
Sat on the land, and covered up the downs,
Rose from his couch, and to the stable hied,
And found the watchers wakeful at their posts.
" Good men," said he, and tipped their palms with
        gold,
" Watch on ; I would once more see Goanveer."
So passed the outer yard, and raised the latch
Upon the door which shut in Guelpho's mare.
A trusty stable-boy sprang to his feet,
And thrust a lantern full in Loosealot's face.
" Who's that ?" he cried ; then, " Guv'nor ! Oh, it's
        you ! "
And Loosealot, " Yes ; how goes the mare to-
        night ? "
" Fust-rate, sir," said the boy ; "and, mark my words,

She'll win like winking." Loosealot said " Umph ! "
The bonny mare stood on three legs and slept
With calm assurance in her close-shut eye.
" Oh," said the Knight again, " boy, go and fetch
A flask you'll find upon my mantelpiece ;
We'll drink the mare's good health before I sleep ;
Hie quickly ! " and the urchin quickly hied.

Then, left alone, did Loosealot begin
Soliloquy. Said he, " The end is come ;
I shall be shamed for ever." And he said,
" Mine be the shame, for I shall have revenge."
With this and with a kick he woke the mare.
She turned her large and lovely eyes on him,
And whinnied as a slave who knows her lord,
Arched high her neck, and rattled at her chain,
And flicked her tail in equine ecstasy.
But Loosealot, keeping *his* eyes turn'd away,
Filled up a bucket to the brim, and put
It 'neath the mare's big mouth, and, stroking down

Her mane, spoke soft, " Drink, pretty creature,
    drink ! "
She, parched with feverish dreams, lower'd her head
To follow his advice, when, quick as thought,
He from his coat-tail pocket did produce
A large blue paper parcel ; opened it,
And in the bucket poured—O sin ! O shame !—
A pound and half of powdered Epsom salts.
With three great gulps the mare drank up the dose,
Stood on three legs again, and fell asleep,
With calm assurance once more in her eye.
And Loosealot, turning up the bucket, sat
On it, and waited for the stable-boy,
Who, coming, brought the flask, and then the twain
Drank to the triumph of swift Goanveer.

The morrow came, as morrows always do—
In prose or poesy it's just the same—
And once again was London's carnival
Inaugurated on the chalky down.

'Twould be to tell an oft-repeated tale

To here put down the humours of the day.

The reader is referred to Mr. Frith,

Or is advised to see them for himself.

Enough that London had turned out to see

The triumph of its favourite, Goanveer.

The world, his wife, and little ones were there,

And swarmed as thick as mites upon ripe cheese.

The Grand Stand an anthropoid ant-hill rose,

And all around the human insects strove.

Guelpho and all his Knights were there ; and he

Was cheered—for not unpopular was he—

When he came forward in the private stand.

And time went on.   Then rang the deep-toned bell

To clear the course, and louder buzzed the hum,

Till it was cleared, and silence fell on all.

Each after each the " cracks " came filing out

From pale-bound paddock, daisy-starred and green ;

And loud shouts greeted Goanveer as she

Pranced proudly by, and Guelpho's hope beat high,

Nor noticed he, nor they, nor any one

Save Loosealot, her dull and watery eye.

Now cantered they ; now sought the starting-post ;

Now came the Derby dog ; then all was still.

But Loosealot had climbed and found a perch

Where rose the highest tier of the Grand Stand ;

And to him, passion pale, there came at last

An ever-rising roar that meant " They're off ! "

And so they were.   A score of matchless steeds

Flashed suddenly like arrows from a bow ;

A vivid rainbow wriggled 'cross the course,

And fourscore hoofs were springing o'er the turf.

The colours tail ; pink shoots past red ; and red

Is lost as orange merges into pink ;

But green is first, and green is Guelpho's hue ;

And hoarsely roars a cry, " The fav'rite wins ! "

On, on they fly, nor seem to touch the turf ;

Slip through the furze, and mount the searching
        hill ;

And pink is hiding orange now, and red

Creeps up past brown, and green—why, green is
    last !

In vain her jockey calls on her; in vain

His spur is in her blood incarnadined ;

Vainly the whip falls on her quivering flank ;

For now the Epsom salts begin to work,

And Loosealot the vile finds his revenge.

Out spread the other horses o'er the slope

Of Tattenham Corner, flying down the hill ;

But Goanveer, with weak and trembling limbs

(The effect of salts when taken to excess),

Scarce kept her legs at all, and hobbled home

An awful twentieth and a shocking last.

Loud rose a clamour; shouting with full voice,

The crowd cried "Traitor!" and edged round the
    mare,

And would have lynched her rider, but they saw

Her shaking haunches and her watery eye ;

Then made for Guelpho's place, and he, all stunn'd

At what had happed, show'd plainly that he was

A victim, not a villain; and they passed,

And drank intensely out of stern despair.

But Loosealot, coming down, put on a look

Of deep regret (he'd won ten thousand quid),

And would have passed; but came the stable-boy,

Sobbing, and shouted, "That's the villain—he!"

Pointing to Loosealot; and Loosealot

Drew back, indignant, and defied the youth;

But he, whipping his hand beneath his coat,

Brought out a piece of paper, and 'twas blue,

Labell'd, moreover, "Epsom Salts," and said,

"This here I found last night in the mare's stall,

Beneath her bucket, after he was gone,

But thought no more of it till when I saw

Our Goanveer break down this side the furze.

He hocuss'd her!"   And Loosealot waxed white,

And tried to see a way, but there was none.

A moment's space, and all the angry crowd

Leapt on him and hurled him headlong, and he fell

Stunn'd, and the policemen bore him off.

And Guelpho knew all, and his heart was sad ;

Not only had he lost the race, and more

In money than is safe to say, but he

Had lost his dearest friend, and been betray'd

By him he reckon'd chiefest of his Knights.

And gloomy he went back to town, and glum,

And very hipp'd.

           But she (the got-at mare)

They took by easy stages to her stall,

And gave her gruel, and bran made in a mash ;

Wrapped her likewise in flannels manifold,

Lest she took cold upon the Epsom salts

And died.

          And so the stately mare abode

For many days, unexercis'd, nor seen

By any save her trainer and his lads,

And chiefly by the little stable-lad,

The 'cute one, who was mention'd heretofore ;

And he, all worshipful, attended her

With all devotion, and with watchful care ;

And loved to sit with her and stroke her neck,

Comb out her tail, and plait her silken mane ;

Polish her hoofs, and keep her skin all sheen ;

And, on occasion, sitting on a tub,

Would sing old songs to her, of strange import ;

And this is one sung by the stable-lad :—

"Late, late, so late ! and dark the night and chill !

Yet if you have a latch-key, ye can enter still ;

    If not too late.   Ye cannot enter now.

"No key have you ?   Then there you see's the rub,

And learning this, to-morrow seek out Chubb ;

    Meanwhile, be off !   Ye cannot enter now.

"No key ? so late ? and dark and chill the night !

How very careless! why, it serves you right.

  Too late, too late! Ye cannot enter now.

"Have we not spoken? Quickly leave our sight!
Don't stand there knocking all the blessed night.

  Too late! d'ye hear? Ye cannot enter now."

So sang the lad while sitting on his tub,
His head upon his hands; but what he meant
The writer does not know. Goanveer neighed,
And flicked her tail as he sang so to her.

And he would moralise and talk to her,
As though she were a mayoress, not a mare;
And he would say, " So ho, my pretty one!
Don't take no powder in your drink again;
Think of your master, of the Coming K——,
How all his heavy losses weigh him down;
And how he has commenced a suit against
Sir Loosealot for heavy damages;

All through your drinking of those nasty salts.
O Goanveer, you foolish, flighty mare ! "

Then Goanveer would toss her head, and paw
The straw with restless foot, and arch her neck,
And look with her large eyes upon the lad.

" Just think, you naughty mare," he would go on,
" What trouble you have caused throughout the land ;
How many youths have robbed their masters' tills,
To pay the money that they lost on you ;
How some, who, ruined quite, have killed them-
        selves ;
How many gone entirely to the bad !
You see you were such a great favourite,
The land was full of you before the race.
Men wore the Goanveer collar, smoked cigars
Called after you, and drank the Goanveer port."

At which the mare did only whinny once,

To whom the lad, still garrulous, again :

" Yes, and the sporting papers went for you,

And all the prophets said that you would win.

They're never right, I know, but in this case

They should have been; but yet you lost the race."

So saying, smack'd her sharply on the flank,

And she pricked up her ears, and with her legs,

Her hind ones, knocked the stable-lad's cap off,

And made him silent for a little space.

So both were still : and ticked the stable-clock,

And rustled in the straw a stable-mouse,

And thought the stable-boy how he one day

Might come to have a mount, and fell asleep.

But Goanveer wondered when her beans would come,

If she would e'er go out to grass again.

Then came a thundering knock against the door,

Which woke the lad, and, pulling back the bolt,

He, dropping nearly, cried, "The Coming K——!"

And Guelpho enter'd, and his face was sad.

So Goanveer heard his step and knew its fall,

And turn'd and rubbed her nose against his hands,

And Guelpho put his arms about her neck,

Laying his face against the satin neck;

And then came silence; thereupon a voice,

Monotonous and hollow, like the Ghost

In Hamlet, but, though changed, the Coming
    K——'s:

" Stayest thou here alone, thou child of sires

And dams most notable in Ruff's Turf Guide ?

Well is it, p'rhaps, thou know'st not what thou'st
    done—

Thy master ruined and his people sold.

I trusted thee, upon thee risked my all,

Not thinking that my Loosealot would be false;

And now, know'st thou from whence I come ?—from
    him,

From entering suits against him for my loss.

And he that did not shun to ' doctor ' thee

Had yet that grace of courtesy in him left,

He spared the action to defend, and let

Judgment go by default, and paid into court

All that he had, save just enough to take

Him to an island of the Southern Seas,

Where stripling Knights of mine love well to roam,

And nature's one vast Agapemone.

Yet think not, Goanveer, I bear thee grudge;

Fear not; I will not send thee to thy death

In knacker's yard, or e'en to cab-rank doom.

Howbeit, thou hast not made my life so sweet

For these few weeks as I could p'rhaps have wish'd,

For thou hast spoilt the purpose of my life;

For I was first of all my line who drew

The errant Knights together under me

In that fair order of my Table Square.

A glorious company, the cream of cream,

Whose object was to make the best of life—

To ride abroad, re-dressing thrice a-day,

To gather scandals at the clubs, to lead

A loosish life—to laze a bit and lush—

To love no woman, but to flirt with all
Until they tired ; for well, indeed, I knew
Of no more dangerous action under heaven
Than marriage, for a Dinner-Table Knight.
It checks his latch-key and his evenings out,
His billiards, and his midnight games at loo ;
It interferes with going 'hind the scenes—
In short, with all that makes the modern Knight.
And all went well till on the turf I went,
Believing thou wouldst fortune bring to me,
And place me higher yet in name and fame.
Then came the shameful act of Loosealot ;
Then came thy breaking down in that great race ;
And now my name's worth nil at Tattersall's,
And all my Knights can curl their lips at me ;
Can say ' I've come a cropper,' and the like,
And all through thee and he—and him I mean—
But slips will happen at a time like this.
Canst wonder I am sad when thus I see
I am contemned amongst my chiefest Knights ?

When I am hinted at in public prints

As being a man who sold the people's race?

But think not, Goanveer, my matchless mare,

Thy lord has wholly lost his love for thee.

Yet must I leave thee to thy shame, for how

Couldst thou be entered for a race again?

The public would not hear of it; nay, more,

Would hoot and hound thee from the racing course,

Being one they had loved, yet one on whom they had

    lost."

He paused, and in the pause the mare rejoiced,

For he relaxed the pressure of his arms:

And, thinking he had done, the mare did neigh

As with delight; but Guelpho spake again:

" Yet, think not that I come to urge thy faults;

I did not come to curse thee, Goanveer;

The wrath which first I felt when thou brok'st down

Is past; it never will again return.

I came to take my last fond leave of thee,

For I shall ne'er run mare or horse again.

O silky mane, with which I used to play

At Hampton!   O most perfect equine form,

And points the like of which no mare yet had

Till thou wast bred!   O fetlocks neater far

Than many a woman's ankles!   O grand hocks

That faltered feebly on that fatal day!

O noble quarters!   And O Goanveer,

I cannot touch thy lips because they froth;

('Twould seem, indeed, as though thy hour was
    scum!)

I cannot take thy tail, lest thou shouldst kick,

Nor shake thy hoof, for that is far from clean;

Yet, Goanveer, I bid thee now good-bye,

And leave thee, feeling yet a love for thee,

As one who first my racing instinct stirr'd;

As one who taught me to abjure the turf.

Hereafter we may meet, I cannot tell;

Thy future may be happy; so I wish.

But this I pray, on no account henceforth

Make mixture of your water : drink it neat ;
I charge thee this.   And now I must go hence ;
Through the thick night I hear the whistle blow
That tells me that my ' special ' waits to start.
Thou wilt stay here awhile, so be at rest ;
But hither shall I never come again,
Or ever pat thy neck, or see thee more.
Good-bye ! "

      And as the Coming K—— let go,
And turned to leave, she with her hoofs let out,
And would have helped him on his mournful way,
But, failing in her reach, he went in peace.
Then, listening till the footsteps had died out,
Rose up the lad, and said, " Well, here's a go !
If he ain't cracked, why blow me tight, that's all.
To come and hug a hoss like that, my heye !
It beats cock-fightin' holler, that it do."

Then she—the mare—lifted her voice and neigh'd,

As she, it seemed, would say, " Exactly so ! "
And, turning, saw the stable-lad, and neigh'd
Again, but this time 'twas for oats ; and he,
Fetching a measure of them, gave her them,
And Goanveer fed, and came upon her rest.

And, as it came to pass, she rested there
Some weeks ; then, sold at Albert Gate, she fell
Into a turfman's hand, who chang'd her name ;
And afterwards she did extremely well,
And gather'd much in stakes and bets for him.
Then she, for her good deeds and her good blood,
And for the speed and pluck that was in her,
And likewise for the name that she had borne,
Was purchased by the Middle Park Stud Co. ;
At Eltham lived : and so, a brood-mare, past
To wheresoever 'tis that horses go.

And Guelpho took his " special " back to town,
And from that night became an altered man.

Henceforward did he lead a different life,

His follies all forsook, and was a King—

Take him all round, as things in this age go,

We may not have so good an one again.

THE END.

Some time hence,

WHEN THE AUTHORS SHALL HAVE ACCOMPLISHED THEIR
PURPOSE, WILL BE PRODUCED

THE SILIAD;

OR,

THE RAPE OF BRITANNIA.

𝔈𝔳𝔢𝔯𝔶 𝔐𝔞𝔫 𝔥𝔦𝔰 𝔬𝔴𝔫 𝔓𝔬𝔢𝔱 ;

OR,

THE INSPIRED SINGER'S RECIPE BOOK.

BY A

NEWDIGATE PRIZEMAN.

Nuper ventosa isthæc et enormis loquacitas animos juvenum ad magna surgentes veluti pestilenti quodam sidere afflavit.—PETRONIUS.

———

THIRD EDITION, ENLARGED.

———

LONDON: SIMPKIN, MARSHALL, & Co.
OXFORD: Thos. SHRIMPTON & SON, BROAD STREET.
1877.

INTRODUCTION.

TO have attempted in former times a work of this description, would have seemed, we cannot deny, to savour either of presumption or of idiotcy, or more probably of both. And rightly. But we live in times of progress. The mystery of yesterday is the common-place of to-day; the Bible, which was Newton's oracle, is Professor Huxley's jest-book; and students at the University now lose a class for not being familiar with opinions which but twenty years ago they would have been expelled for dreaming of. Everything is moving onward swiftly and satisfactorily; and if, when we have made all faiths fail, we can only contrive to silence the British Association, and so make all knowledge vanish away, there will lack nothing but the presence of a perfect charity to turn the nineteenth century into a complete kingdom of heaven. Amongst changes, then, so great and so hopeful—amongst the discoveries of the rights of women, the infallibility of the Pope, and the physical basis of life, it may well be doubted if the great fathers of· ancient song would find, if they could come back to us, anything out of the way or ludicrous in a recipe-book for concocting poetry.

Some, indeed, object that poetry is not progressive. But on what grounds this assertion is based, it is not possible to conjecture. Poetry is as much progressive as anything else in these days of progress. Free-thought

itself shews scarcely more strikingly those
three great stages which mark advance and
movement. For poetry, like Free-thought,
was first a work of inspiration, secondly of
science, and lastly now of trick. At its first
stage it was open to only here and there a
genius; at its next to all intelligent men; and
at its third to all the human race. Thus, just
as there is no boy now, but can throw stones at
the windows which Bishop Colenso has broken,
so there is scarcely even a young lady but can
raïse flowers from the seed stolen out of Mr.
T*nn*s*n's garden.

And surely, whatever, in this its course of
change, poetry may have lost in quality, is
more than made up for by what it has gained
in quantity. For, in the first place, it is far
pleasanter to the tastes of a scientific generation,
to understand how to make bad poetry than to

wonder at good; and secondly, as the end of poetry is pleasure, that we should make it each for ourselves is the very utmost that we can desire, since it is a fact in which we all agree, that nobody's verses can please a man so much as his own.

OF THE NATURE OF POETRY.

POETRY as practised by the latest masters, is the art of expressing what is too foolish, too profane, or too indecent to be expressed in any other way. And thus, just as a consummate cook will prepare a most delicate repast out of the most poor materials, so will the modern poet concoct us a most popular poem from the weakest emotions, and the most tiresome platitudes. The only difference is, that the cook would prefer good materials if he could get them, whilst the modern poet will take the bad from choice. As far, however, as the nature of materials goes, those which the two artists work with are the same—*viz.*, animals, vegetables, and spirits. It was the practice of Shakespeare and other earlier masters to make use of all these together, mixing them in various proportions. But the moderns have found that it is better and far easier to employ each separately. Thus Mr. Sw*nb*rne uses very little else but animal matter in the composition of his dishes, which it must be confessed are somewhat unwholesome in consequence; whilst the late Mr. Wordsworth, on the contrary, confined himself almost exclusively to the confection of primrose pudding, and flint soup, flavoured with the lesser celandine, and only now and then a beggar-boy boiled down in it to give it a colour. The robins and drowned lambs which he was wont to use, when an additional piquancy was needed, were employed so sparingly that they did not destroy in the least the general vegetable tone of his productions; and these form in consequence an unimpeachable Lenten diet. It is difficult to know what to say of Mr. T*nn*s*n, as the milk and water of which his books are composed chiefly, make it almost impossible to discover what was the original nature of the materials he has boiled down in it. Mr. Shelley, too, is perhaps somewhat embarrassing to classify; as, though spirits are what he affected most, he made use of a large amount of vegetable matter also. We shall be probably not far wrong in describing his material as a kind of methyllated spirits, or pure psychic alcohol, strongly tinctured with the barks of trees, and rendered below proof by a quantity of sea-water.

In this division of the poets, however, into animalists, spiritualists, and vegetarians, we must not be discouraged by any such difficulties as these; but must bear in mind that in whatever manner we may neatly classify anything, the exceptions and special cases will always far outnumber those to which our rule applies.

But in fact, at present, mere theory may be set entirely aside; for although in case of action, the making and adhering to a theory may be the surest guide to inconsistency and absurdity, in poetry these results can be obtained without such aid.

The following recipes, compiled from a careful analysis of the best authors, will be found, we trust, efficient guides for the composition of genuine poems. But the tyro must bear always in mind that there is no royal road to anything, and that not even the most explicit directions will make a poet all at once of even the most fatuous, the most sentimental, or the most profane.

RECIPES.

HE following are arranged somewhat in the order in which the student is recommended to begin his efforts. About the more elaborate ones, which come later, he may use his own discretion as to which he will try first; but he must previously have had some training in the simpler compositions, with which we deal before all others. These form as it were a kind of palæstra of folly, a very short training in which will suffice to break down that stiffness and self-respect in the soul, which is so incompatible with modern poetry. Taking, therefore, the silliest and commonest of all kinds of verse, and the one whose sentiments come most readily to hand in vulgar minds, we begin with directions,

————————

HOW TO MAKE AN ORDINARY LOVE POEM.

Take two large and tender human hearts, which match one another perfectly. Arrange these close together, but preserve them from actual contact by placing between them some cruel barrier. Wound them both in several places, and insert through the openings thus made a fine stuffing of wild yearnings, hopeless tenderness, and a general admiration for stars. Then completely cover up one heart with a sufficient quantity of chill churchyard mould,

which may be garnished according to taste
with dank waving weeds or tender violets:
and promptly break over it the other heart.

HOW TO MAKE A PATHETIC MARINE POEM.

This kind of poem has the advantage of
being easily produced, yet being at the same
time pleasing, and not unwholesome. As, too,
it admits of no variety, the chance of going
wrong in it is very small. Take one midnight
storm, and one fisherman's family, which, if
the poem is to be a real success, should be as
large and as hungry as possible, and must
contain at least one innocent infant. Place
this last in a cradle, with the mother singing
over it, being careful that the babe be dream-
ing of angels, or else smiling sweetly. Stir

the father well up in the storm until he disap-
pears. Then get ready immediately a quantity
of cruel crawling foam, in which serve up the
father directly on his re-appearance, which is
sure to take place in an hour or two, in the
dull red morning. This done, a charming
saline effervescence will take place amongst
the remainder of the family. Pile up the
agony to suit the palate, and the poem will
be ready for perusal.

HOW TO MAKE AN EPIC POEM LIKE
MR. T*NN*S*N.

*(The following, apart from its intrinsic utility, forms in
itself a great literary curiosity, being the original directions
from which the Poet Laureate composed the Arthurian Idylls.)*

To compose an epic, some writers instruct
us first to catch our hero. As, however, Mr.
Carlyle is the only person on record who has

ever performed this feat, it will be best for the
rest of mankind to be content with the nearest
approach to a hero available, namely a prig.
These animals are very plentiful, and easy to
catch, as they delight in being run after.
There are however many different kinds, not
all equally fit for the present purpose, and
amongst which it is very necessary to select
the right one. Thus, for instance, there is the
scientific and atheistical prig, who may be
frequently observed eluding notice between the
covers of the "Westminster Review;" the
Anglican prig, who is often caught exposing
himself in the "Guardian;" the Ultramontane
prig, who abounds in the "Dublin Review;"
the scholarly prig, who twitters among the
leaves of the "Academy;" and the Evangelical
prig, who converts the heathen, and drinks
port wine. None of these, and least of all the

last, will serve for the central figure, in the present class of poem. The only one entirely suitable is the blameless variety. Take, then, one blameless prig. Set him upright in the middle of a round table, and place beside him a beautiful wife, who cannot abide prigs. Add to these one marred goodly man; and tie the three together in a bundle with a link or two of Destiny. Proceed, next, to surround this group with a large number of men and women of the nineteenth century, in fancy-ball costume, flavoured with a great many very possible vices, and a few impossible virtues. Stir these briskly about for two volumes, to the great annoyance of the blameless prig, who is, however, to be kept carefully below swearing-point, for the whole time. If he once boils over into any natural action or exclamation, he is forthwith worthless, and you must get another. Next break the wife's reputation into small pieces; and dust them well over the blameless prig. Then take a few vials of tribulation and wrath, and empty these generally over the whole ingredients of your poem : and, taking the sword of the heathen, cut into small pieces the greater part of your minor characters. Then wound slightly the head of the blameless prig; remove him suddenly from the table, and keep in a cool barge for future use.

HOW TO MAKE A POEM LIKE MR. M*TTH*W A*N*LD.

Take one soulful of involuntary unbelief, which has been previously well flavoured with self-satisfied despair. Add to this one beautiful text of Scripture. Mix these well together ; and as soon as ebullition commences, grate in finely a few regretful allusions to the New Testament and the Lake of Tiberias, one con- stellation of stars, half-a-dozen allusions to the nineteenth century, one to Goethe, one to Mont Blanc, or the Lake of Geneva ; and one also, if possible, to some personal bereave- ment. Flavour the whole with a mouthful of " faiths " and " infinites," and a mixed mouth- ful of " passions," " finites," and " yearnings." This class of poem is concluded usually with some question, about which we have to observe only that it shall be impossible to answer.

HOW TO MAKE AN IMITATION OF MR. BR*WN*NG.

Take rather a coarse view of things in general. In the midst of this, place a man

and a woman, her and her ankles, tastefully
arranged on a slice of Italy, or the country
about Pornic. Cut an opening across the breast
of each, until the soul becomes visible, but be
very careful that none of the body be lost
during the operation. Pour into each breast
as much as it will hold of the new strong wine
of love: and, for fear they should take cold by
exposure, cover them quickly up with a quantity
of obscure classical quotations, a few familiar
allusions to an unknown period of history, and
a half-destroyed fresco by an early master,
varied every now and then with a reference
to the fugues or toccatas of a quite-forgotten
composer.

If the poem be still intelligible, take a pen
and remove carefully all the necessary particles.

HOW TO MAKE A MODERN PRE-RAPHAELITE POEM.

Take a packet of fine selected early English, containing no words but such as are obsolete and unintelligible. Pour this into about double the quantity of entirely new English, which must have never been used before, and which you must compose yourself, fresh as it is wanted. Mix these together thoroughly till they assume a colour quite different from any tongue that was ever spoken, and the material will be ready for use.

Determine the number of stanzas of which your poem shall consist, and select a corresponding number of the most archaic or most peculiar words in your vocabulary, allotting one of these to each stanza; and pour in the other words round them, until the entire poem is filled in.

This kind of composition is usually cast in shapes. These, though not numerous—amounting in all to something under a dozen—it would take too long to describe minutely here : and a short visit to Mr. ——'s shop in King street, where they are kept in stock, would explain the whole of them. A favourite one, however, is. the following, which is of very easy construction. Take three damozels, dressed in straight night-gowns. Pull their hair-pins out, and let their hair tumble all about their shoulders. A few stars may be sprinkled into this with advantage. Place an aureole about the head of each, and give each a lily in her hand, about half the size of herself. Bend their necks all different ways, and set them in a row before a stone wall, with an apple-tree between each, and some large flowers at their feet. Trees and flowers of the right sort are very plentiful in church windows. When you have arranged all these objects rightly, take a cast of them in the softest part of your brain, and pour in your word-composition as above described.

This kind of poem is much improved by what is called a burden. This consists of a few jingling words, generally of an archaic character, about which we have only to be careful that they have no reference to the subject of the poem they are to ornament. They are inserted without variation between the stanzas.

In conclusion we would remark to beginners that this sort of composition must be attempted only in a perfectly vacant atmosphere; so that no grains of common-sense may injure the work whilst in progress.

HOW TO MAKE A NARRATIVE POEM LIKE
MR. M*RR*S.

Take about sixty pages-full of the same
word-mixture as that described in the preced-
ing; and dilute it with a double quantity of
mild modern Anglo-Saxon. Pour this com-
position into two vessels of equal size, and into
one of these empty a small mythological story.
If this does not put your readers to sleep soon
enough, add to it the rest of the language in
the remaining vessel.

HOW TO MAKE A SPASMODIC POEM LIKE
MR. R*B*RT B*CH*N*N.

This is a very troublesome kind of poem to
make, as it requires more effort and straining
than any other. You are yourself also one of

the principal ingredients; and it is well, there-
fore, to warn you, before you use yourself for
this purpose, that you will be good for nothing
else after you have done so. The other ingre-
dients, which, like those of a quack medicine,
are mostly gathered under the moon, or in a
planetary hour, must be first prepared as
follows.

For a poem of a hundred lines (enough to
satisfy one person) take ten verses-full of star-
dew, twenty-five verses-full of the tides of
night, fifteen of passion-pale proud women,
well idealized, five of starry ice-crystals, ten of
dank grass and night-shade, fifteen of aching
solitude, and twenty of frost-silvered mountain
peaks, bubbling runnels, and the sea. Into
these put the moon, with stars *ad libitum;* and
sprinkle the whole over with broken panes of
a Grub-street garret window. This done, your

next step is to prepare *yourself*.   The simplest
way is to proceed as follows.

Take yourself, and make eyes at it in the
glass until you think it looks like Keats, or
the "Boy Chatterton."   Then take an infinite
yearning to be a poet, and a profound con-
viction that you never can be one, and try to
stifle the latter.   This you will not be able to
do.   The aim of the endeavour is to make the
conviction restive.   Then put the two together
into yourself; and the conviction will immedi-
ately begin to splutter, and disturb you.   This
you will mistake for the struggles of genius,
and you will shortly after be thrown into the
most violent convulsions.   As soon as you feel
these beginning, jump into the middle of your
other ingredients; your movements will before
long whip them up into an opaque froth,
which as soon as you are tired out and become

quiet, will settle, and leave your head protruding from the centre. Sprinkle the whole with imitation heart's-blood, and serve.

HOW TO MAKE A SATANIC POEM, LIKE THE LATE LORD BYRON.

(This recipe is inserted for the benefit of those poets who desire to attain what is called originality. This is only to be got by following some model of a past generation, which has ceased to be made use of by the public at large. We do not however recommend this course, feeling sure that all writers in the end will derive far more real satisfaction from producing fashionable, than original verses; which two things it is impossible to do at the same time.)

Take a couple of fine deadly sins; and let them hang before your eyes until they become racy. Then take them down, dissect them, and stew them for some time in a solution of weak remorse; after which they are to be devilled with mock-despair.

HOW TO MAKE A PATRIOTIC POEM LIKE MR. SW*NB*RNE.

Take one blaspheming patriot, who has been hung or buried for some time, together with the oppressed country belonging to him. Soak these in a quantity of rotten sentiment, till they are completely sodden; and in the mean while get ready an indefinite number of Christian kings and priests. Kick these till they are nearly dead; add copiously broken fragments of the Catholic church, and mix all together. Place them in a heap upon the oppressed country; season plentifully with very coarse expressions; and on the top carefully arrange your patriot, garnished with laurel or with parsley: surround with artificial hopes for the future, which are never meant to be tasted. This kind of poem is cooked in verbiage, flavoured with Liberty, the taste of which is much heightened by the introduction of a few high gods, and the game of Fortune. The amount of verbiage which Liberty is capable of flavouring, is practically infinite.

CONCLUSION.

E regret to have to offer this work to the public in its present incomplete state, the whole of that part treating in detail of the most recent section of modern English poetry, *viz.*, the blasphemous and the obscene, being completely wanting. It was found necessary to issue this from an eminent publishing firm in Holywell street, Strand, where, by an unforeseen casualty, the entire first edition was seized by the police, and is at present in the hands of the Society for the Suppression of Vice. We incline however to trust that this loss will have but little effect; as indecency and profanity are things in which, even to the dullest, external instruction is a luxury, rather than a necessity. Those of our readers, who, either from sense, self-respect, or other circumstances, are in need of a special training in these subjects, will find excellent professors of them in any public-house, during the late hours of the evening; where the whole sum and substance of the fieriest school of modern poetry is delivered nightly; needing only a little dressing and flavouring with artificial English to turn it into very excellent verse.

Titles in this Series

Criticism: General, Poetic, and Dramatic

1. Alfred Austin. THE POETRY OF THE PERIOD. 1870

2. Robert Buchanan. A LOOK ROUND LITERATURE. 1887

3. John William Cole. THE LIFE AND THEATRICAL TIMES OF CHARLES KEAN, F.S.A. 1859. (In two volumes)

4. E. S. Dallas. POETICS: AN ESSAY ON POETRY. 1852

5. E. S. Dallas. THE GAY SCIENCE. 1866

6. H. Buxton Forman. OUR LIVING POETS: AN ESSAY IN CRITICISM. 1871

7. Walter Hamilton. THE AESTHETIC MOVEMENT IN ENGLAND, third edition, 1882

8. R. H. Horne, editor. A NEW SPIRIT OF THE AGE, second edition. 1844. (In two volumes)

9. Madge Kendall. THE DRAMA. 1884. with DRA-MATIC OPINIONS. 1890

10. Joseph A. Knight. A HISTORY OF THE STAGE DURING THE VICTORIAN ERA. 1901

11. Lord William Pitt Lennox. PLAYS, PLAYERS, AND PLAYHOUSES AT HOME AND ABROAD. 1881. (In two volumes)

12. Robert James Mann. TENNYSON'S "MAUD" VINDICATED: AN EXPLANATORY ESSAY. 1856

13. Mowbray Morris. ESSAYS IN THEATRICAL CRITICISM. 1882

14. Henry Neville. THE STAGE: ITS PAST AND PRESENT IN RELATION TO FINE ART. 1875

15. "Q" [Thomas Purnell]. DRAMATISTS OF THE PRESENT DAY. 1871

16. Walter Raleigh. STYLE. 1897

17. William Caldwell Roscoe. POEMS AND ESSAYS (volume two, ESSAYS, only). 1860

18. Clement Scott. THE DRAMA OF YESTERDAY & TODAY. 1899. (In two volumes)

19. James Field Stanfield. AN ESSAY ON THE STUDY AND COMPOSITION OF BIOGRAPHY. 1813

Parody, Satire, Literary Controversy, and Curiosa

20. Edward Bulwer-Lytton. THE NEW TIMON. 1846.

with Algernon Charles Swinburne. SPECIMENS OF MODERN POETS. THE HEPTALOGIA, OR THE SEVEN AGAINST SENSE. 1880. with Algernon Charles Swinburne. "DISGUST: A DRAMATIC MONOLOGUE." 1898

21. [William E. Aytoun and Theodore Martin.] THE BOOK OF BALLADS: EDITED BY BON GAULTIER. 1845. with [William E. Aytoun.] FERMILIAN: OR THE STUDENT OF BADAJOZ: A SPASMODIC TRAGEDY BY T. PERCY JONES. 1854

22. James Carnegie. JONAS FISHER: A POEM IN BROWN AND WHITE. 1875. with [A. C. Swinburne.] THE DEVIL'S DUE: A LETTER TO THE EDITOR OF "THE EXAMINER." BY THOMAS MAITLAND. 1875

23. Philip James Bailey. THE AGE; A COLLOQUIAL SATIRE. 1858

24. [W. C. Bennett.] ANTI-MAUD. 1856. with [Eustace Clare Grenville Murray.] THE COMING K———. 1873. with [W. H. Mallock.] EVERY MAN HIS OWN POET. 1877

25. [John Burley Waring.] POEMS INSPIRED BY CERTAIN PICTURES AT THE ART TREASURES EXHIBITION, MANCHESTER. 1857. with [Anon.] THE LAUGHTER OF THE MUSES. 1869

26. Robert Buchanan. THE FLESHLY SCHOOL OF POETRY AND OTHER PHENOMENA OF THE DAY. 1872.

with Algernon Charles Swinburne. UNDER THE
MICROSCOPE. 1872

27. J. Rutter. THE NINETEENTH CENTURY, A POEM,
IN TWENTY-NINE CANTOS. 1900

Collections of Critical Essays

28. William E. Fredeman, editor. VICTORIAN PREFACES
AND INTRODUCTIONS: A FACSIMILE COLLECTION.
1986

29. Ira Bruce Nadel, editor. VICTORIAN FICTION: A
COLLECTION OF ESSAYS FROM THE PERIOD. 1986

30. Ira Bruce Nadel, editor. VICTORIAN BIOGRAPHY:
A COLLECTION OF ESSAYS FROM THE PERIOD.
1986

31. John F. Stasny, editor. VICTORIAN POETRY: A
COLLECTION OF ESSAYS FROM THE PERIOD. 1986

32. William E. Fredeman, editor. THE VICTORIAN
POETS: AN ALPHABETICAL COMPILATION OF THE
BIO-CRITICAL INTRODUCTIONS TO THE VICTO-
RIAN POETS FROM A. H. MILES'S "THE POETS AND
POETRY OF THE NINETEENTH CENTURY." 1986